INTENTIONAL GRANDMOTHERING...

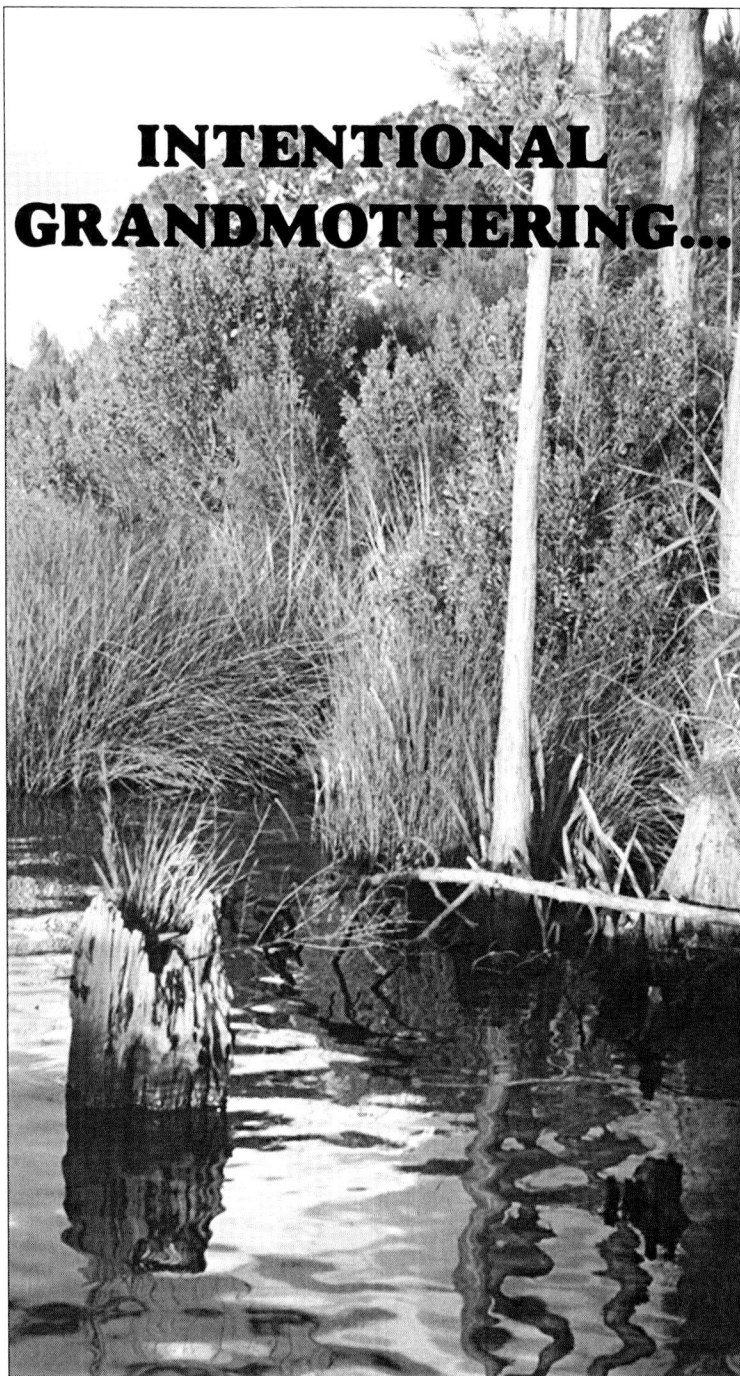

Books from
Path of Potential

The Becoming Intentional People Series:

INTENTIONAL GRANDMOTHERING... CHOOSING THE LIFE PHILOSOPHY THAT WORKS FOR ALL CHILDREN IN THE WORLD

ADVANCING OUR HUMANNESS... CHOOSING A PATH OF CONGRUENCE WITH INTENT

The Desert Series:

WORK FOR ALL CHILDREN

AT THIS TIME OF POTENTIAL

WHO WILL SPEAK FOR EARTH? Reflections on Securing Energy from a Life of the Whole Perspective

DEVELOPING PLANETARY ETHICS; The Urgent Work of Today's Generation

Compilations:

THE OIL SPILL PAPERS; Creating a New Path, a Path that Works for All Children

GIFTS OF THE SPIRIT; Experiencing Death and Loss from the Perspective of Potential

Other Writings from Path of Potential
The Path of Potential Library:
www.pathofpotential.org

~

To order books, go to the Path of Potential website, or call:
Melody Fraser, The Mail Suite, 1-800-818-6177 or 1-970-241-8973

INTENTIONAL GRANDMOTHERING...

*Choosing the Life Philosophy
that
Works for All Children in the World*

Terry P Anderson
Sandra Maslow Smith

Path of
Potential

Intentional Grandmothering...

PHOTOGRAPHY
Candi Clark
Sandra Maslow Smith
Shannon Marie Smith

COVER, BOOK DESIGN, and GRAPHICS
Candi Clark

PRINTING
Precision Printing
Grand Junction, CO 81501 • www.ppgj.com

PUBLISHER
Path of Potential
P.O. Box 4058 • Grand Junction, CO 81502 USA
www.pathofpotential.org

AUTHORS
Terry P. Anderson
Sandra Maslow Smith

First printing – 2013
Printed in the United States of America
SFI® Certified (Sustainable Forestry Initiative) Acid Free

Path of
Potential *is a trademark of TS Potential, LLC*
ISBN-10: 0-9760139-7-5
ISBN-13: 978-0-9760139-7-6

TABLE OF CONTENTS

This book is all about life, the ongoing intended unfolding of life... the eternalizing of life on and through earth.

This book is all about choosing the life philosophy that works for all children in the world... a life philosophy that sees intentional grandmothering as process... the process of the grandmothering of life, the life of all children and the whole of life within which the children – all the children in the world – live.

What follows here is writing that has emerged from ongoing reflection and intentional dialoguing along the path of potential... the path of intent... the path of our potential to be and become fully, truly and wholly human... as intended.

We have found that reading this book aloud in gatherings of two or more brings spirit to the process and life to the seeing and understanding called for at this time.

THE LIVING PHILOSOPHY
AND THE WORK

To be Clear...

To be clear, these writings, these reflections, the ongoing intentional dialoguing are all about – of and from – philosophy. Whereas, given the nature of the work before us, some of the subject matter dealt with is common to theology/religion; this is not theology – reasoned interpretation of the word; rather, this is about a particular philosophy – a life of the whole, essence-based philosophy...

A philosophy referred to as the living philosophy of potential.

A philosophy anchored in Source: One Source, all else instruments; and emanating from and through the Source is intent and intended ways of working within and through life – the ongoing, intentional, upward unfolding of life on and through earth.

A philosophy that focuses on becoming, on realizing our potential to become fully and truly human... which in turn requires of us the taking on of a life of the whole perspective, a perspective that both transcends the limitations of, and fully embraces the truths within our current human centered perspective.

And ultimately, a philosophy aimed at enabling our returning to following a path of intent, a path sourced in original intent, an unfolding intentional path of life... a way of being and becoming an intentional people.

Through the development and processing of this philosophy, some seeing and understandings have emerged that are critical to now – to the work of now. To begin with: The perspective we hold, where we start our thinking from, determines the path we take, the direction we move in, what we move towards, what we move away from. Thus the significance of the shift from human centered to a life of the whole centered perspective, a perspective that allows us to see ourselves, and especially all our children, as woven within the processes of life... not environmentally, ecologically separated from, but fully and truly woven within the unfolding intentional processes of life. And to see ourselves having, like all of life's members, work and role with regard to the sustaining and ongoingness of life, the eternalizing of life on and through the earth: to act in accord with Thy will... to live in accord with *the Father's command of eternal life – on earth as in heaven* (Jn12:50; Mt6:10).

Real shifts, upward shifts, involve – call upon – both heart and mind, not as separate phenomenon, but rather as systemic expressions of the whole... the whole of the work before us, the whole of the work now called for along the path of intent, the path of our potential... the whole reflected in opening our hearts to the mother's command, *Work for all my children in the world...* the whole reflected in developing the mind – the seeing and understanding – required for bringing the world of our making into congruence with the world of intent... and the wholeness of heart and mind that enables our moving towards wholeness, away from that which divides.

A necessary reality of our entering into life on earth is the development of a world view – a view of the world that encompasses both the visible and the invisible aspects of our world. How we see the world greatly influences our thoughts and actions regarding philosophy, science and religion; all of which in turn greatly influence our culture – the development and ways of our culture. How we process the visible and invisible aspects of our world is grounded in our perspective and directionally organized by mind – the particular mind of the time. A human centered perspective naturally brings with it the urges of instinct – survival, procreation, etc., of the species – and the application of intellect, the development of intelligence for personal, human advantage. The dominant mind has been the reasoning mind of existence... dealing with both the visible and the invisible through reasoned interpretation, seeking structure to have meaning, and pursuing segmentation and reductionism to become knowledgeable – expert, an authoritative source in particular arenas. All of which seek to serve humanity both in terms of existence – our having a good life – and in terms of afterlife – the invisible segment of life.

Now... at this time... given the children's reality – the reality and obvious direction of the world of our making – and the work before us, we are being called upon to access and develop the intuitive mind of essence... to see and come from essence – patterns of intent – versus starting our thinking from existential structures... to orient ourselves to realizing potential versus segmented problem solving. A reality and work requiring the seeing of process, the seeking of wholeness... the nature of directional organizing now required, a directional organizing not possible through the reasoning mind of existence acting in and of itself; but one which requires the reasoning mind of existence to carry out, to be manifested in the world of our making. A directional organizing that brings forth a yin and yang complementarity between the intuitive mind of essence and the reasoning mind of existence... providing of course that the yin of intuition and the yang of reason come from, share in, and are disciplined about the truths of Source:

One Source, all else instruments...

Emanating from and through the Source is intent and

intended ways of working of life and of ourselves within life…

A wholeness within, a systemic way of working, which makes possible – moves us in the direction of – becoming intentional people: a people with hearts open to all children in the world, a people developing and processing a world view through a wholistic mind of intent – an intentional systemic harmonious working of intuition and reason.

Finally, on the path of intent, the initiating process of our returning to the path of intent is the repotentializing of ethics, in particular, intentional ethics, ethics sourced in the intentional ways of life. To contemplate, to dialogue, the subject of ethics requires some consideration of morality – the complementary companion of ethics. In one sort of way we can see morality in terms of consequences – not only within the present human community, but also within the context of afterlife, and associated with that, the notions of salvation, being saved, sinfulness, forgiveness, etc. On the other hand, intentional ethics deal with the ongoingness, the eternalizing of life on and through the earth, and the willfulness on our part to not only not interfere with, but rather nourish and honor life's systems and processes, nourish and honor intent and intended ways of working of life – the whole of life… a willfulness that reflects our commitment to see and understand intent – to start our thinking from that versus gaining manipulative knowledge for bringing about that which reflects our will, our desire. Associated with intentional ethics is not so much the notion of forgiveness, of wiping the slate clean; but rather the notion of redemption, of our returning to the path of intent… returning and taking up our work and role in the ongoingness of life… our moving towards nourishing life, towards realizing potential… our moving away from self-centered extraction.

The living philosophy of potential is all about life... the here and unfolding now... and about work... work as the means to manifest spirit, the accessing and manifesting of spirit, spirit essential to the eternalizing of life... work requiring we see life as process, Christ as process... and work requiring the process of intentional dialoguing. All of which begins (or not) with the development of serious intent...

From the perspective of the living philosophy of potential, earth, life and our entry into earthly life came about through serious intent of the Source.

We, being unique among life's creatures, were created in the image and likeness of the Source... and thus have the inherent capacity to take on and come from serious intent.

Through serious intent we can transcend ordinary life limitation and become fully and truly human... true instruments of the Source.

Now Needed: A Willful "YES"

And so... the realization of the potential of Mary's "Yes" began...

> The wedding celebration runs out of wine... that which nourishes the festivity.

> Mary says to Jesus, It is time... time to begin your work. Jesus says, But I am not ready. Mary calls the servants and says, Do as he tells you. Jesus turns water into wine... wine not previously present... a new wine, the best wine.

> A pattern is broken... good wine, the best wine is served at the end, rather than at the beginning. A new wine signaling the beginning of a new era... a new way... a pattern shift brought about by new structuring... the structuring of all-inclusive love... the intentional all-inclusive love of the Source... a new wine, a new mind intended to become common... a practiced way.

And now we have the mother's command: *Work for all my children in the world...*

> It is the children... it is in and through the children that oneness and wholeness become possible... it is through the children that essence and existence can harmonize in intended ways... it is through our working for all the children in the world that all-inclusive love can enter.

> And so, what is needed now is a willful "Yes"... the yes of the intuition of wholeness... a yes that begins the realization of the potential of women in life... in the intended unfolding of life... the eternalizing of life on this earth... an ongoingness of life that requires, now requires work for all children, work for all my children in the world... requires the taking up of the work, perhaps with some hesitation, some reluc-

tance, but nevertheless hearing and embracing the mother's command – the life eternalizing command of *Work for all my children in the world.*

The Work Now before Us

The mother's command – *Work for all my children in the world* – speaks to and from intuition – the intuition of wholeness... a speaking, the hearing of which is received by the heart and organized by the community mind of essence... the mind that seeks and begins with wholeness... the mind that is disturbed by artificial notions of separation, fractionation – notions inhibiting intended oneness and wholeness. It is the mind that sees all children within and through the love of inclusivity... and the one that sees all children as living human beings, as from and of the Life, inseparably of and from life, woven within life such that the children's wellbeing, their future, their ongoingness, and the ongoingness of life – the vitality and viability of life – are one and the same... a mind that focuses not so much on the ending of life, on escaping from life; but rather on the eternalizing of life... *the coming of the kingdom* (Mt6:10). The mind of essence sees all children as equal in essence, equal in spirit and spirituality.

The mother's command, the heart opening command of our mother – *Work for all my children in the world* – is the voice of the intuition of wholeness... the innermost voice of our advancing humanness... that which calls us, leads us in the direction of now... the direction of the particular shift, the upward step, a real shift in our humanness, that which is required for the intended unfolding... the unfolding of now... the unfolding of life... the unfolding of our potential to be and become fully and truly human... an unfolding that requires of us the taking on of a life of the whole perspective.

This is the voice of work, the work that is now before us, the work that is behind the stirring more and more of us are innerly experiencing... work reflecting and illuminating a significant shift, a change in our way of thinking... shifting from the mind of existence to the community mind of essence... shifting from instinct and survival to intuition and becoming. The mind of existence stirred by this voice of work asks, What is my work? What am I to do? The voice-stirred mind of essence seeks clarity as to What is the work? What is our work with regard to that? What do I, what do we need to be and become? And ultimately, what is the work of humanity, the human community within the larger whole of life, the work that reflects both our living-ness and our humanness? ...our humanness being the unique aspect of our livingness.

This is the voice, the commanding voice that both calls us and invites us into the work... an invitation that requires a conscious choice... an authentic "Yes"... an exercising of free will... a manifesting of spirit... a full expression and inner realization of our humanness, of our human poten-tial... a true taste of what it means to be human – really and truly human. The mother's command, the heart opening command of our mother, to come, to join in, to work for all my children in the world; the truth of this, the wholeness, the oneness of this; is truth enough... "proof" enough... "proof" enough to each and all who say "Yes," who come together to take up this work.

Seeing work as truth – a central truth of our existence, a central truth of life, the ongoingness of life – is the initiat-ing place, the birthing place for the now process of advanc-ing our humanness... the particular process for the particu-lar shift being called for... the shift at the heart of the unfolding that is active, actively stirring us now. This process of now, like all advancing humanness processes, starts with the heart; thus, at this time, the mother's com-mand, the command of our mother to *work for all children in the world*... and by those with serious intent, the seeking and the developing of the mind – the community mind of essence – the mind that not only encompasses the heart opening command of our mother, but also embraces the Father's command... the command made clear by Christ. *The Father's command is eternal life* (Jn12:50)... the process of eternalizing life lifted up in the familiar going forward prayer also given to us by Christ:

Our Father, who art in heaven, hallowed be Thy name; Thy kingdom come, Thy will be done on earth as it is in heaven (Mt6:9-10)... a prayer that reflects intentionality in life and in life's ways on this earth... the very earth we live upon.

Thus the work now before us:

> *Work for all my children in the world.*

> *Bring the world of our making into congruence with the living world of intent.*

Which brings us to the going forward question, the narrow gate of our time:

> *Do we have the heart for the work now before us?*

> *Do we have the will to develop the mind the work requires?*

Part 1

CLEARLY SEEING THE REALITY BEFORE US

The Children's Reality

This writing is emerging from conversations and understandings that are coalescing around the children of the world... a coalescing no doubt led by the mother's command,

Work for all my children in the world,

and influenced by the forward path work of creating the active presence of a "work for all children in the world" culture. All of which contribute to the seeing and understanding of the children's reality... the reality with regard to the current world of our making; and the reality with regard to our potential, our human potential... the potential within, the potential for us as a community to become fully and truly human... a realizing of potential that requires our making life real, and demands the transcending of the inherent limitations and the artificial pursuits of the reasoning mind of existence.

As we read, reflect upon and dialogue what is written, it is important and quite helpful to hold several things in mind, beginning with the common law, an intentional truth, of earthly life:

The perspective we hold, where we start our thinking from,
determines the path we take, the direction we move in,
what we move towards, what we move away from.

Another intentional truth is:

If love is not present in the process,
love will not be present in the outcomes.

Love – that which we are not the source of, but rather

intended instruments for its entry into the working of the world – is what will make possible the inner shift – the step change – from our current ways to that which works for all children… the inner advancement of our humanness that moves us in the direction of bringing the world of our making into congruence with the world of intent.

Whereas, from the mind of existence, we see real shifts – true step change – in terms of external manifestations, external structuring brought about through evolutionary processes; when it comes to the advancing of our humanness – step change along the path of our becoming fully and truly human – we look to inner unfolding, an inner unfolding led by increasingly whole perspectives… the taking on, absorbing, living from perspectives that encapsulate larger and larger wholes. The progression of ourselves, the intentional advancing of our humanness, is grounded in oneness and wholeness: Oneness with the Source; wholeness within self, within community, within humanity, within the whole of life… each of the previous progressions in wholeness seemingly requiring the next unfolding to be itself fully developed, to be fully realized.

Common within the Christian community is the notion that a central message of Christ was that God cared about the whole of humanity, not just a select few… a notion reflecting the inclusive love that Christ brought into the world. Now we can see the necessity for a life of the whole perspective to fully realize wholeness within humanity… life, our livingness, being the shared characteristic, an intentional commonality, present within all of humanity. We, each and all, come from a common Source, from the Life, the Source of life.

This progressional advancing of our humanness has some similarity to the developmental processes of an individual

20

(e.g., self, family, community, etc.). However, at this time, community is the smallest whole. It is wholeness – within humanity, within the people of earth; it is all the children, not the segmented few – that sets the course, the direction we need to move in… direction and work that require the accessing and development of the mind of essence… the mind that looks to the intuition of wholeness for seeing and understanding the wisdom of intent and intended ways of working of life.

An authentic path forward requires clear understanding of the current – current ground, current ways, what is at work, etc. – sufficient clarity to keep us from pursuits and a path that seem different, that evoke within, a sense of hope; but in reality are just different expressions of what is, what was; not manifestations of what needs to be created.

And so, with the critical eye of conscience, we can engage in a reflective seeing of current reality… current reality for the children and for life, the life of the whole within which they are intentionally and inseparably woven. Let us then reflect upon the world of our making, the world within which the children live… our increasingly artificial world, a world disconnected from the Life – the Source of life – and isolating itself from the Spirit, the Spirit that enters through life… a world that more and more reflects the people's loss of faith in life… in the Life. A world that would evoke from Mother Teresa, the comment that the spiritual poverty in the Western World is greater than any poverty she experienced in India.[1] A world where manipulative knowledge is favored over understanding of and congruence with intended ways of working… a world where we pursue not so much congruence with intent and intended ways, but rather that which we wish, that which is a demonstration of our capacity to subdue, to have power over, to bring about and shape the world and our ways of living congruent with our image... a world where manipulative knowledge, cleverness, smartness, legalness, are given status – status through successful ends, status over ethics, ethical ways, status over wholistic ways, over ways that work for all children. A world of diminishing vitality and viability for the whole of life... a world organized around the energies and materials of existence... a world engaged in a downward cascading process of coarser and coarser energies... pursuing products and processes that lead us in the direction of increased mechanicalness – less conscious, more reactive... products and processes that are bringing into being a generation that lacks the capacity to be present in the moment – an emerging age of haste, continual busyness and unguided reason... an age driven by human possibilities – pursuits and demonstrations of the possible – pursuing the possible, with little regard for human potential, for advancing our humanness (not to be confused with increased power and control)... little regard for becoming fully and truly human, an intended becoming often obscured by the partial perspectives of returning and salvation. A people bolstered by notions of salvation, of being saved, of being rescued, swept away from the trials and tribulations of life – of existence-based life. A people free from obligations, intentional ethics with regard to the ongoingness of life... a people more caught up with gaining eternal life than taking up the intended work of eternalizing life on and through this earth. A people following a path of extraction, extracting, self-serving pursuits which are themselves emboldened by an underlying philosophy of "I am saved; He is coming; what happens to life on earth is irrelevant." Concerns over hazardous consequences to essential life processes of earth are believed unwarranted and burdensome to our ongoing success, our personal pursuit and achievement of happiness... happiness being viewed as a high – if not the highest – moral imperative of our pursuits on this earth... earth – after all – was created for man; not man created for earth, nor earth created for life to have a place to enter into the working of the creation; no, earth – life on earth – was created for man to manipulate, to shape, to form, to subdue in congruence with his wishes, his desire, his pleasure. A philosophy and orientation that leads the thinking of a people and culture, a philosophy that is more focused on extracting than adding value... on the pursuing of impressions of goodness, of being good versus pursuing the right and good – right for the whole of humanity, good for the whole of life. This is the world of our making... a world not moving in the direction of increasing congruence with the world of intent, the intent of the Source; but rather a world that emerges from and operates within an illusion of our being the source. This, the world of our making, is the current reality... the reality of the children... the world within which they live.

Wow, certainly not a very comforting picture, some disturbing images, yet very real images. But then comfort is not what conscience is about – the seeking of that. Rather conscience is the seeking of critical clarity... critical clarity being not so much judgmental, but more seeing critically, bringing forth unvarnished realness regarding current reality, current path... the path we are on, the path we have been on. Yes, undoubtedly, there are manifestations of efforts aimed at congruency with intent, with the reality of our being "living" creatures, creatures who exist within life, not outside of life, not separate from the whole of life. These happenings will come to the fore, as we begin to see and understand our forward path. The purpose of this conscience led reflection was and is to gain confronting clarity and certainty with regard to what is, with regard to where we are at.

Continuing on with our aim to share images and understanding, not for the purpose of creating a winning argument, but rather for the purpose of enabling dialogue and processes of deepening understanding... deepening understanding of what is at work here, in particular, what is behind, what is the source of what is at work here. The energizing, organizing source of the world of our making, that which is leading the way along our current path, is the mind of existence... the mind that organizes itself around the external – that which is before us, the sensory accessible, the provable, factual – the physical, the material and energy aspects of existence, the stuff of our life... that which ultimately creates within our society an existence-based material oriented culture – a culture of things, stuff, possessions and status with regard to such.

The mind of existence needs structure to have meaning. Whereas the intuitive mind of essence looks to wholeness and process, the mind of existence looks to structure to have meaning – structure in terms of things, structure in terms of hierarchy, etc. We can see this at work in the early days – the first couple hundred years or so – of Christianity. That which started out as process – in many ways a "kitchen table process," highly influenced and often led by the women – shifted in the direction of structure, a shift coincidental with the entry of the elite – the people of means and power – into the process. What emerged was a hierarchical structuring, the establishing of power and control... a structural emerging that was further enhanced by the problem seeking, problem solving patterns of reason. The mind of existence naturally looks to reason to carry out its pursuits... reason with its segmenting, fractionating processes... reason which looks not so much to generate wholeness, but rather to segment, separate the whole into parts, often seeking, through segmentation, the accessing and gaining of power and control over... the pursuit of being in power, of having power and having control, power and control over others, over one's life, one's destiny.

Continuing with the path of Christianity, we can see this segmenting pattern at work. Present at the time, through existence-based Greek philosophy, was the notion of divided self, the divided self of man... a notion embraced by Augustine and many others. Most simply the divided self of man was separated into two parts, the higher self and the lower self... the higher self being the rational self, the controllable self... the higher self being the domain of the soul... the lower self being the domain of the life energies, sex, other "animal" energies, etc. – the irrational, the uncontrollable. The higher self was attributed to the male; the lower self to the female. And it was commonly thought that it was the duty of the higher self to be in control over the lower self. Patterns of being in control became embedded in the ways of Christianity. The rational man, of necessity was to have authority over the irrational.

The rational man – the reasoning mind of existence, the pursuit of the winning argument, the pursuit of the convincing, undeniable proof – not only became woven within Christianity, but embedded within the emerging Western culture as well.

Looking further at the natural way of working of the reasoning mind of existence, we see not only the more familiar patterns of analysis, segmentation and fractionation – the breaking of things into smaller and smaller parts, seeking more and more knowledge of more and more segments – but also the virtue of focus – the capacity to focus on task, to pursue goals and objectives, often relentlessly. Thus that which thrives on division can readily become single minded, even in ways that can become unreasonable, irrational in themselves... and clearly through reflection, unwise. Not uncommonly, we can see in this process the shedding of significant aspects of that which we are pursuing, significant aspects like purpose, intent, wholeness, integrity, ethics, for example; and more and more commonly the reduction of conscience to that which is legal... to conformance to legality, legality being the highest recognized necessity – that which we must follow.

Exploring this shedding process is enhanced through re-connecting to the intentional working of earthly life: *The perspective we hold, where we start our thinking from, determines the path we take, the direction we move in, what we move towards, what we move away from.* And remembering that the reasoning mind of existence provides the ordering and organizing process for the commonly held segmented, human centered perspective... segmented, often hierarchically (me and mine versus all), with regards to the children, for example. Continuing then... common start points for our thinking are economics, legality and rights, often used together in various combinations and sequences. We can look at a not uncommon pattern throughout much of business today (business being the name we give to how we as human beings organize to generate and realize value. If we were bees, we would probably look to the way of the hive – the beingness of it, its organizing processes), the pattern of starting our thinking from economics – often more specifically financial extraction – which quickly becomes the focus of our reasoning power and which allows and enables the shedding process – the losing sight of purpose, intent, integrity with regard to employees, community, life, etc. – and the pursuit, through cleverness, smartness, etc., of "legal" means to leverage the gains of a few... with legality itself looked at from multiple viewpoints – as a necessary restraint, a burdensome boundary, a favorable rule, often "rules of the game." We can see similar patterns today – economically led patterns – in the fields of education, medicine, religion, governance, sports, etc. One of the realities of our ways of working is that we cannot get to value, much less virtue, by starting with economics; rather getting to value calls for organizing around virtue/value and generating reciprocally nourishing economics[2] around that... reciprocal nourishment being the essence process – the intended way of working of life – an essential process readily visible as we see and reflect upon such things as pollination, soil making, etc.

And so, whereas the economic led thinking patterns of today are, shall we say "intuitively obvious," they are not necessarily restricted to the present. We can see the influence of economic start points, pursuits of power and control, active in the arguments and debates that took place in the Spanish courts following Columbus' discovery of America. The debate was centered around whether or not the indigenous people – the people living here when we arrived – had a soul... an important truth, given that our obligations to beings that possessed a soul were much greater and very different from those without souls. And therefore, in terms of economics and power over, our utilization of and dealing with such people would be greatly influenced. Apparently, for a decade or so, it was successfully argued that the "live here's" did indeed have a soul; however, further argument – "higher order proof" – prevailed in terms of, "No, no soul present."

Perhaps a bit of a pause would be useful here. Remembering our conversations have the aim of clear seeing with regard to the world of our making, to the path we have been on, and what is at work in that regard, we have looked to the working of conscience to gain critical clarity... and are aware of the naturalness of this seeing arousing within, some judgmentalness as well as a bit of negative energy. Important for us is to not act on or act from this, but rather acknowledge it in an observing, nonattached sort of way... a way that allows us to continue to develop clarity, and not be sidetracked – tempting as it may be. A friend of mine once counseled, "See it as part of the process"... useful advice to our staying with our intent.

Continuing on with our conversations, we find ourselves imaging the emergence of the age of enlightenment – the period in which the rational man, through science, burst forth on the scene... burst forth with a new vision for the world... a vision we could bring about, a shaping and forming of earth and life on earth through our images of what could be... transcending human limitations, bending the material and energy aspects of earthly existence to create for ourselves the previously unattainable. It is natural for us to want to move up platforms of existence... and now with this new pathway of human possibility, of the humanly possible, we could see more carefree, less difficult, less troublesome ways of living and doing. Useful here is to hold in mind that the human potential – our potential to become fully and truly human, a path of advancing humanness – and human possibilities are not automatically one and the same, nor even automatically complementary... a reality that brings forth the emerging question of our pursuits along the path of human possibility, a questioning regarding their effect on humanness, essential humanness: Are they advancing or diminishing humanness?

The patterns of the reasoning mind of existence became, at this time of enlightenment, much more vivid, organized, enlivened, more forceful... and thus more influential. The patterns of debate and argument, of proof and facts, of segmentation and fractionation, of structure, linearity and step-by-step methodology were and ongoingly are integrated into our ways of living and doing... giving strength and life to the existence-based, the material nature of the culture of today.

Reflecting on the natural tendencies of power and control –

28

not just power and control over the "human weaknesses" within self, but beyond self as well – we see an inherent hazard within the pursuits and achievement of power and control is the experiential illusion of our being the source... a process of disconnecting ourselves from the Source, the Source of life, the Source of all... and from the truth of our instrumentality: *One Source, all else instruments.*

In one sort of way, we can see this at work when the enlightenment began to flourish, especially as science and technology extended – took us beyond the limitations of – human sensory power (telescopic seeing, observing the heavens, the movements of the heavenly bodies, for example). Now a factual, provable knowledge was obtainable... a human possibility that brought with it source-based competition, debate and argument; in an ironic sort of way, the reasoning mind of existence was arguing within itself. The classic example of course being Copernicus' telescope and the revelation that the earth orbited the sun, not the previously held – by religious authority – truth that the sun orbited the earth. At essence, what was at work here was reasoned interpretation of structure – the very thing the existential mind requires to have meaning. On the one hand we had reasoned interpretation of the structure, the structure we call "the word," and the particular organized collective of that – the Bible. On the other hand we had reasoned interpretation of the works, the structures of creation. Thus began the ongoing "arm wrestling" with regard to being the authoritative source – the "previously authorized" interpreters wrestling with the new commanders of facts and proof: who sets the direction, the course of humanity; who determines what is real, what is myth, what is fact – what is factual, provable.

Furthering our conversation with this example, we can see present today an ongoing manifestation of conflict and debate within the reasoning mind of existence... within the competition for gaining and sustaining literal/factual dominance – power over. Present within Christianity and within science is a conflict between the literal word and factual evolution. Many within Christianity, within salvation theology, hold the creation story – Adam and Eve, our fall from grace, our need to be saved, etc. – as the central core, the critical ground, the fundamental basis for Christianity – for Christ coming to earth, for Christian religion. Within science, the theory of evolution – the structural relatedness, progression, evolving of the species, the environmental influences upon this progression, and the millions of years through which this has occurred – is central to, the critical ground, the fundamental basis for science. In both cases it is held that the diminishment, the discounting, the discrediting of what is central would eliminate the ground upon which they stand... disenabling their ability to function, to carry out their work.

These arguments – their presence and ongoingness – are a central aspect of the children's reality – the reality of now. Momentary contemplation brings to mind some thoughts in this regard. There is hazard here in religion becoming a myth... a factually un-substantiate-able myth; with the reasoned interpretations of theology becoming less relevant to what is present before us, essential truths and teachings may be obscured in the dust of argument. And there is hazard in the science led path of human possibility increasingly disconnecting us from the Source, taking us off the advancing humanness path of our potential – the path of intent – and leading in directions that diminish humanness, increase mechanicalness... creating structures that turn us away from spirit and towards addictive energies of existence, and ultimately to an externally driven, existence-based culture.

Whereas it is conscience that we look to, to gain clarity of current path; it is intuition we look to for guidance with regard to our forward path. It is useful to look at intuition, what it was experiencing along the path the reasoning mind of existence was bringing forth. We know from our experience that intuition – the processes and processing of intuition – is commonly, if not always, a source of frustration for reason – the linear sequential processes of reason. The rapid imagery and clear conclusions that emerge, without following prescribed (linear) procedures, are particularly disconcerting. At the time of the rational enlightenment, women were considered to be the repository for intuition... perhaps indicated by the common expression, "women's intuition." And so, as the thought base for the age of reason became more structured, more procedural, more linear, etc., the component fields of science, engineering, mathematics, etc., commonly were considered the domain of the male... creating an effective barrier and separation between male and female... not unlike that established by the reasoning mind of existence within Christian religion. So, in one sense, the two competing processes for authoritative power and control were organized structurally to diminish women's access... perhaps reflecting ongoing traces of the divided – higher and lower – self. And beyond the obvious consequences to the women, there were significant consequences/impacts on human potential, on our becoming fully and truly human, as intended; that being the setting aside, so to speak, of intuition and thus wisdom... the wisdom of experience and the wisdom of intent and intended ways of working. On the one hand, we sustained some orientation towards the returning process illuminated by salvation organized religion, and on the other hand we had an energized pathway of human possibility impacting our daily life... both of which, separately or together, lacked the wholeness and completeness of thought to seriously and authentically illuminate the path of human potential – the becoming path of intent... the here and unfolding now path of advancing our humanness... a path that embraces the truth that *if love is not present in the process, love will not be present in the outcomes*... wholeness, of course, being the domain of intuition – not the nature implied by "the whole is equal to the sum of its parts," but the nature of "seeing" that comes about through reflective processing, the imaging of intent, intended ways of working.

It is natural and unavoidable to contemplate the children's reality without bringing to mind women's reality... the women's reality at the core of the women's movement that came to life a while back, yet not so long ago, in that many who joined in this process are still actively alive. It is beyond the scope of this writing to deal with women's reality in the depth necessary for clear imagery... imagery that may be helpful in the work of today... the work for all children in the world... the work of creating an active presence of a "work for all children" culture... work that understands community to be the smallest whole. Several things come to mind. Engaging women's reality was a necessary unfolding, a critical preparation for engaging the children's reality. Intuition – intuitive processes within our culture, our existence grounded culture – is diminishing. The reasoning mind of existence is forcibly entering more and more of our essential systems and processes, including business, education, governance, family, etc. That which enables and calls upon intuition is being shed, often through thinking that begins with economics, legality, and rights – "my right(s)" to carry out particular desired activities without regard for the larger whole of community, of life, etc. Gadgetry technology is distracting, perhaps addictively seducing, more and more of us away from the real, more and more in the direction of the artificial... away from life, intended ways of life.

However, there is an awakening, a stirring of conscience

with regard to current ways, the unfolding destiny of our current path, the unfolding future of the children... a growing recognition of the necessity to think a new way... a radically new way. Evidence of this is showing up in the field of medicine where some are emphasizing understanding of intended ways of working – versus manipulative knowledge – within the healing of injuries; some are seeking to understand what is taking place within swelling – swelling that causes discomfort – seeking congruence with natural healing versus treating symptoms. In the world of business – operating from a principle of our being accountable for structures we bring into existence, and following a philosophy of bringing the world of our making into congruence with the world of intent – some are seeking to extend recycling processes to include repotentializing processes, processes that require an understanding of virtue – the essence pattern of intent – with regard to the materials we use. For example, the repotentialization of various plastics and polymers (e.g., plastic bottles, nylon carpeting) reflects the gaining of value from the essence pattern of intent of petroleum... the virtue of petroleum being perpetual products, everlasting products. It is enlightening to see that which took earth millions of years to create is intended to be a source of everlasting structures... a radically new way of thinking versus the current focus on BTU's[3] and combustion processes for petroleum. This radical way of thinking holds as an anchoring point, the inseparability of the ongoing wellbeing of the children from the whole of life, their inseparability from the vitality and viability of the essential life processes of earth... leading to pursuits that embrace the truth of the children being intentionally created as members in the community of life.

Out from this stirring has emerged the understanding of the necessity for developing the mind of essence and accessing, through the intuition of wholeness, the wisdom of intent.

Thus the need now is not for the continued diminishment of intuition, but rather the inspiriting of intuition, the repotentialization of intuition, an inspiriting of intuition to the intuition of wholeness... the intuition of wholeness being essential to the accessing of the wisdom of intent, the seeing and taking up of our work... our intended work as living human beings.

1. Wooding, D. *The day Mother Teresa told me, "Your Poverty is Greater than Ours."* ANS, July 4, 2010. Lake Forest, California: ASSIST News Service, 2010.
2. Anderson, T.P. *Current Reality: The Loss of our Humanness... A Real Risk of Today.* www.pathofpotential.org
3. British Thermal Unit

Our Human Reality

We have seen our human reality from the perspective of problem, from a focus on human weaknesses, human failings; we have created theologies that have a central theme of our weaknesses, of our sinfulness… theologies that have within, elements of fear, processes of control. Likewise we have created technologies that seek to lift us up from the burdens and drudgeries of life… technologies, emerging from science, that seek to extend and transcend human limitations, overcome – conquer – disease and illness, and pursue the overcoming of what is often considered the greatest of human failings – death itself. In one sort of way, we have continued to struggle with the enemy within, the enemy without… an orientation that creates within our culture a language, a way of speaking, and a way of organizing, around the concept of war – the war against, the war of for and against – language and ways that naturally evoke the coarse energies of meanness, anger, violence, hatred… and processes that encourage, induce, and enable divisiveness and fear… out from which emerges the world of our making – the energy field within which the children exist. And given our cultural capability, our work ethic that allows us to separate our way of making a living from our life outside of work, we can make our living, accumulate wealth in ways that diminish humanness, exploit the children, threaten the vitality of life itself… and being a rational people, we can create the rationale – the justification for our ways… and ultimately create a culture that honors success – material, positional success attained in these ways.

It is an interesting thing to observe this combination of the problem seeking, problem solving patterns of reason being organized by the mind of existence… which come together in structure, in the need for the existential mind to have structure to have meaning. Within the mind of existence,

it is structure, not process, that is the source of meaning…
it is structure that becomes both the ends and the means…
it is structure that becomes "sacred," that which must pre-
vail, take precedence over… it is structure that demands
obedience and loyalty… and in times of discord, it is structure – the power and control within that – that becomes
superordinate, superordinate even to the wellbeing of the
children.

The mind of existence starts with what is, and naturally
starts with ourselves – our condition, our existence, the
human condition, our desire to escape the burdens and
struggles of life, our need to be rescued, to be saved; thus the
need at this time to transcend the inherent limitations of
the mind of existence, to develop the mind of essence… a
mind that starts with Source and instrument, with intent
and intended ways of working… a mind that accepts that at
the core of our human reality is that we are of and from
life… a mind that sees our potential and sees the hope for
all children lies along and within a path of life… a real path
of life, life made real through congruence with intent of the
Source – through a culture that reflects intent, has a process
orientation, and aims of oneness and wholeness.

Reflecting further on the path of life, the way of life – the
upward unfolding intent of life – we gain added imagery of
the here and unfolding now reality of the children. Life
dynamically and dramatically unfolds before us… a thrust-
ful forward process – a before us rather than a behind us
process. Inherent within the children, the young adult, is
the purposeful work of making life real[4]… a sorting out of
the artificial from the real… separating what was from what
is emerging, intentionally emerging now… a spirit led
process of seeing and understanding that which they are
moving into… an adventurous process not only essential to
each and all, but to the ongoingness of life as well. The

36

children, the young adult, they too have before them work, role, purpose, instrumentality in the intentional working of life... soul building, spirit manifesting work, work that reciprocally nourishes the Source, the Life. All of which at this time of now, requires clarity regarding the original path, the path of intent... and regarding that which is seeking to emerge now. Yet, given the external power of culture – the power to externally define and inhibit intrinsic expression – and the artificial culture, the culture of artificiality that engulfs them; it is probably not surprising that so many would choose to drop out – turn away from the current – perhaps unable to create realness, real paths for themselves.... paths that reflect wisdom – the wisdom of intent... paths that would create within – innerly – the experience of work... real work, work in harmony with life, work that advances our humanness, intentional work. In one sort of way, the village – the current way of the village – is disenabling, dispiriting essential processes of the children, of life. Here again, reflecting on the way of life brings to the fore a contrast between the mind of existence and the mind of essence. The mind of existence sees the structuring notion of plan – often in terms of "God has a plan; He will move us about as he sees fit." The mind of essence sees intent, intentionality with regard to the ongoing unfolding... intent that calls upon and requires instrumentality – instruments... which in turn requires a conscious "Yes" on our part – a true exercise of free will, real work on our part.

These path-of-life reflections bring to mind some words of Christ... *I am the way, the truth, and the life... Come follow me... Be ye like children* (Jn14:6; Mk8:34; Mt18:3).

Perhaps life will not be – in the near future, perhaps never – an easy, a comfortable path; but life is the real path – the original, the intentional, the ongoing path of our potential, the truth and the way of our becoming fully and truly human… a path of processes of Spirit, of Spirit entering, spirit manifesting… a path of intentional possibilities, intentional possibilities made real through love entering the process, through the *love that makes all things possible* (Mt19:26; 1Jn4:8).

Central to this way of life is work, the reciprocally nourishing work required for the eternalizing of life on and through earth. Work is not only central to life, but is the intended common experience of the members of life… not only singularly, but within community – particular communities within the larger community, within the larger whole of life. We can see this at work within the pollinators (e.g., bees, hummingbirds, etc.), and the soil makers (e.g., worms, ants, etc.). This reality of reciprocally nourishing work is an intentional reality of ourselves, of humanity, of the human community that is fully encompassed within – not separate from – the larger community, the whole of life. An understanding of our work and role within life is emerging… an understanding that will become more whole, more complete as we move in the direction of becoming an intentional – authentic – people of life… people organized by the community mind of essence… a mind that engages reason – the problem solving capacity of reason – to bring the world of our making into congruence with the world of intent… the mind that exercises free will – conscious choice (that which is viewed as separating us, a distinction from, other life species) – in ways that reflect the intended ways of working of life… willful, conscious choices that move us away from the artificial and towards the real… processes that will turn us away from the inner pride of what we can do and move us towards fully appreciating the beauty of the intended ways of working of the creation of life… an appreciation that will inspirit our efforts to understand and enable intended ways… intentional manifestations of co-creating versus manipulation for self-serving ends.

4. Anderson, T.P. and S.M. Smith. *Work for All Children*, pp. 9-13. Grand Junction, Colorado: Path of Potential, 2008. (http://pathofpotential.org/wp/?p=765).

Faith – Faith in Life

Having faith in life, we would see our ways of living and our ways of making a living becoming a truer and truer reflection of the way of life, the ways of life, the reciprocally nourishing ways of life… working in ways where the work itself is following a pattern of intent… a means for accessing and manifesting spirit… a new source of meaning, a way of adding value and realizing value… a way of advancing humanness… a way of sustaining and eternalizing life. Coming from faith in life and understanding intended ways – seeking congruence with that – would have status within a culture of life; manipulative knowledge, particularly that which is used for self-serving extraction would be shunned, would be a taboo versus that which is looked up to.

Faith in life is the faith of oneness and wholeness. It is the faith that fully embraces the whole of the Source, the whole of creation; enfolded within faith in life are the processes of returning and becoming, not as separate or segmented processes, but rather inseparable processes of the whole of life… intended, intentional processes.

Reflecting on our ways, it has been common to see God in the light of returning, to focus on behaviors in that regard, and acknowledge the necessity of grace for gaining return… grace being the particular returning pattern emerging from all-inclusive love, the love of the Source, the love Christ brought into the world. All of the truths of this segment of focus are fully enfolded into, actively present in a faith in life… a faith anchored in the Source, the Source of all, in the intent and intended ways of the Source… intended ways, not hidden or inaccessible, but rather fully available to us through the accessing of wisdom, the intuitive accessing of wisdom… the process of seeing and understanding intent and intended ways of working. Thus what has been a commonly held limited perspective of God, now becomes a more whole, a more fully embracing of the truth of the Source... the Source of life, the Source of each and all... the Source of *love through which all things are possible* (Mt19:26; 1Jn4:8).

Faith in life is a faith that not only embraces the truths of returning, but more wholistically embraces the inclusive love and compassion of equality lifted up by Christ; thus making possible wholeness within our fragmented humanity and the creating of cultures and processes that work for all children in the world... a wholeness that enables oneness with Source, and a manifestation of oneness within ourselves – one people of earth – thus common humanness, common livingness – the central core of ourselves – can truly become the anchoring start point for our thinking... a start point that itself is anchored in, comes from a life of the whole perspective, versus the currently active segmenting start points – e.g., ideologies, theologies, gender, race, ethnicity, etc.

Having faith in life, living and working in the way of life, we can live our values within work as well as outside of work; thus inside the energy field, the culture of work, of business, we can be innerly whole, innerly true, working in ethical ways, ways that are reciprocally nourishing, ways that are intentional.

Reflecting on reciprocal nourishment, the essence character of the way of life; and the reality that each and all, each community has intended work with regard to the sustaining and perpetuation of life on earth; we can see a more wholistic image of the command to go forth and multiply. Earth was created to have a place for life to enter into the working of the creation; man was brought into life through earth. As a member of life, man has work and role with regard to life; life is intended to flourish, to multiply upon this earth. Humankind, through the mind of essence – the intuitive mind of essence – guiding reasoning, can authentically participate – fulfill its role – in the flourishing and multiplying of life on this earth.

Inherent within the developmental processes of the children as they work towards adulthood is the purposeful work of making life real.[4] This work naturally reflects the dynamic, unfolding – not static or fixed – way of life. Life is a going forward process – emerges and unfolds before us. Thus the children are entering the emerging unfolding, not the previous unfolding – that which was emerging then. This is a pattern along the path of life, a pattern of the way of life... a pattern of realness.

This work of making life real brings forth some images of the children's reality – current reality... reality in the context of this artificial construct – this world of our making. Images of a back eddy, a circular side stream appear... a side stream separate from, at best tangentially connected to, the stream of life... experiencing the physical, energetic aspects of life, but outside of the spirit nourishing waters of truth and wholeness... separated from the fullness of life, connected to the Source with the partial thread of the returning process. This then is the reality within which the young adult is seeking to make life real. Within this dynamic are cultural pulls of an existence-based culture and its patterns of existence-based motivations with regard to goals and objectives... motivations, goals and objectives from the artificial constructs of then, which quite naturally create discord – generational discord... a reality that becomes more complex as the naturally driven pursuits of the youth to explore various energy fields lifts up for them the coarse energy fields of today, and the equally seductive mechanical energies related to manipulation and accessing of knowl-ledge, in particular the electronic pathways available. No doubt pretty tricky waters to swim within and navigate through… a complexity that brings forth images of the Gordian knot… and through reflection some clarity of the common experience, the human reality with regard to energies we, each and all, have within… a complexity of energies, longings, leanings, etc. The common focus in this regard is control/power over and/or fear of; perhaps there is more hope in first understanding these energies, then wisely dealing with them.

---

4. Anderson, T.P. and S.M. Smith. *Work for All Children*, pp. 9-13. Grand Junction, Colorado: Path of Potential, 2008. (http://pathofpotential.org/wp/?p=765).

The Perspective We Hold

The perspective we hold, where we start our thinking from, determines the path we take, the direction we move in, what we move towards, what we move away from…

We do not own the land, the air, or the water… rather we borrow them from our grandchildren, all the children of the world… and the whole of life as well. This is the true debt of our time… and, given our path and ways, an increasingly burdensome and unforgiveable debt…

When it comes to diminishing the vitality of earthly life… the ongoingness of life… capitalism, socialism, communism, etc., are equally effective… each lacking intentional wholeness, and inclusive completeness of approach.

We as free choice beings, can – with intentional processing – choose to walk a path of harmony with intent and with life's intended ways of working… or we can use the powers of reason and reasoning to pursue manipulative knowledge to bring about a world of our making that is congruent with our wishes, our desires, our will. The first would be a way of manifesting faith in the intent of the Source… the latter a manifestation of the arrogance of self…

How can we own a mountain, the seashore, the desert, the rolling plains… for these belong to the Creator, the Source of all. Ours is not to own, but rather to live and work in harmonious appreciation with… in ever increasing awe of the unfolding beauty and ways of creation.

A common experience as we think about perspective is to see a multitude – the presence of many perspectives… a variety among people, and, at times, within ourselves. However, with a bit of contemplative reflection, we can see that behind the multitude is a commonly held perspective – a human centered perspective. Less common, but the perspective called for at this time – that which needs to be commonly held – is a life of the whole perspective... a shifting from our current human centered perspective to a life of the whole perspective... a perspective that not only embraces the whole of the truth of ourselves, but the intentional wholeness of life itself.

The Organizing Power of Philosophy

Within our way of working, it is philosophy, the organizing power of philosophy, that is at the core of our manifestations – what we create, what we bring into existence. Beliefs, values, truths, premises, etc., are made real – lived out – through philosophy. Within philosophy is the willfulness of discipline, and ultimately that which we become a disciple of. We have seen the organizing power of philosophy as we have reflected upon the influence of the divided self – the rational/the irrational self – the central core brought forth through the reasoning mind of existence… a processing that not only characterized our ways of the last two thousand or so years (perhaps long before that), but also characterized how we look at, see and perceive all that that has come before… how we have seen and recorded history… the history of mankind, the evolutionary history of earth, earthly life… a story of life that has been his story. The predominant trace within our path, as we have seen and told the story, has been his story – stories of dedication, bravery, leading, saving, rescuing, etc. Of late, through the women's movement, women's reality, we have come to see – be enriched by – her story… and the stories of other peoples, native peoples, other segments of our segmented human perspective. What is emerging now is our story, the intentional story of humankind – the whole of humanity… a story that begins with wholeness… wholeness not as an expression of a collection of segments or a summing up of parts, but rather coming from wholeness, a perspective of wholeness, a perspective made possible through oneness, oneness with Source, oneness of Source.

Our story is a story that begins at the beginning, but is now at this time, engaging in a new unfolding… a new unfolding that is being stirred from within… an unfolding that requires – calls for – an inner developmental shift within ourselves – within the whole of humanity… a developmental shift that follows the pattern of the previous with the taking on, the embracing of a larger whole perspective, a life of the whole perspective… a perspective anchored in the living philosophy of potential, a philosophy that looks to the intuition of wholeness to access the wisdom of intent, and follows the organizing patterns of the community mind of essence… the processing mind of essence.

This developmental shift repotentializes – makes active and present – the truths of our origin… the truths of original intent… the truths that are the central core of the living philosophy of potential… the core out from which emerges not only our story; but the children's reality, the emerging making life real story… the moving away from the artificial construct of our making, and the making of life real – the weaving of the intended ways of life within our ways, our culture, our systems…

Perhaps a bit of recapitulation of the living philosophy of potential would enable our imagery, our conversational reflection. The living philosophy of potential has its origin in the beginning, in the original intent… that which preceded the unintended act of disobedience, preceded that which necessitated our being saved, rescued, redeemed. It – the living philosophy of potential – emerges from the process mind of essence and through the intuition of wholeness. So it begins…

Earth was created for life to have a place to enter into the working of the creation. Humankind was created for the living earth, the unfolding and eternalizing of life on and through earth. Earth was not created for man – for man to exploit, for man to diminish the vitality of. We are intentionally, not accidentally, living beings – members in the larger community of life. Reciprocal nourishment is the essential process – the essence way – of life, of life within and between its members. As living beings – true members of life – we too are intended to live and interact in reciprocally nourishing ways, not only within our human community, but within the larger whole of life as well.

There is a Source; we are not the source, but rather, like all of life, intended instruments… instruments that have real work and roles within life – within the steady state, the run up, and the everlasting processes of life.

●

A helpful image for us has been the dot and the line… the dot being the Source – the hierarchical Source. The line being all else – individuals, hierarchical structures, organizations, etc. – all else being equal, equal in essence, equal in significance. There is a natural tendency, aided by the reasoning mind of existence, for us to seek and create hierarchy – status and position – within and along the line… an illusion of insignificance when viewed in the context of the Source – one Source above all else. What is real is work and role; all have real work, real roles to carry out… work and roles reflecting intent and intended ways of working… work and roles that acknowledge the significance of life, and our significance within life.

Wisdom is present to creation; she has access to intent and intended ways of working… the intent and intended ways of life… of the Source of life… of the Life. We, as living human beings, are neither asked nor called to take up work and ways we cannot see or understand;

that which is needed, the seeing and understanding required, is accessible through the intuition of wholeness. Whereas we, as individuals, have had access to wisdom, access to the Spirit through intuition, an accessing through self for developing soul and manifesting spirit – for becoming wholly; what is asked for now is a similar process, but one where community – not the self – is the smallest whole; thus dialoguing, reflectively dialoguing from a life of the whole perspective – a new way of ordering and organizing our ways of living and working – is required. It is in this process of reflective dialoguing – coming from a life of the whole perspective, carried out in regard to particular work and emerging realities – that the community mind of essence is created... the energy field, so to speak, of the process mind of essence... the processing of essence which is particularly relevant to the run-up and everlasting processes of life. Whereas the reasoning mind of existence commonly looks to brain, smartness, etc., the processing mind of essence looks to the intuition of wholeness, the wisdom of intended ways – harmony with that – versus manipulative knowledge. We can get a notion of the processing mind by observing bees as they engage in the "dance" that accompanies the return to the hive of bees bearing nectar, out from which an understanding of magnitude, direction, etc., emerges... an understanding that apparently exceeds the "brain" capacity of a single bee. Within the context of the reasoning mind of existence, with its emphasis on structuring and knowledge, there are examples of individualized capacity (the expert, the really smart, etc., those we look to for advice, to lead, etc.), especially with regard to existence – issues and problems anchored in existence. The processing mind of essence, whereby it requires particular discipline within individuals, is in reality created in the moment, within the dialoguing.

In terms of discipline, within a culture of existence – a culture sourced in the reasoning mind of existence – debate and argument, particularly winning arguments are expected and are inherent to the process. Within the dialoguing processes of the mind of essence, image building versus debate and argument are central; in fact, debate and argument have a negative effect on the creation and sustaining of the necessary energy field.

And so, getting back to our story, our intentional story... our returning to the unfolding path of life, a path of intended ways... a story which is unfolding, unfolding in accord with the image of the Source, the ongoing Source of life... our story of a time of a developmental shift, an innerly shift in being... an advancement in humanness along the path of our becoming fully and truly human... an advancement that focuses on human potential versus human weaknesses... an advancement which calls for our bringing the world of our making into congruence with the world of intent... a process of turning our backs on the artificial, and moving in the direction of making life real – real for ourselves, real for the children; getting back to our intentional story...

This returning to – this repotentialization of ourselves within – the path of original intent is made possible through the impulse, the manifested spirit of Christ entering into the life processes of earth. A spirit manifested is available forever to all. Now is the time of realization of the Spirit made real – accessible and actively present through the redemption work of Christ. The time for the reestablishing of ourselves on the original path of intent, the initiation of which we see in the words, *I am the way and the truth and the life* (Jn14:6) – the going forward proclamation of Christ. The returning work – the reconnecting of ourselves to the returning process, returning to the Source – having been accomplished, now we could take up becoming ways and work; we too – it is now possible for us – could pursue the realization of our human potential (recall humanly possible and human potential being quite different)... our human potential to take up ways and work that move us along the life path of becoming fully and truly human – the manifestation of *Come follow me* (Mk8:34).

It is interesting that from our point of view, salvation – being saved – became so dominant that the life path of becoming became somewhat obscured, an obscuring enabled by our pursuit of human possibilities... a focusing on the returning path that seemed to have been organized by our "hearing" the words, "I am the way and the truth and the savior." However, now at this time, the forward proclamation of "life"... the Life, from Life, of life, is becoming fully awake within us; we are more and more, with increased depth and understanding, being awakened – becoming more conscious of this truth, *this truth of life*... an awakening that most certainly – through the community mind of essence, a life of the whole perspective, and the intuition of wholeness – will bring new seeing and understanding with regard to *the way* and *the truth* as well. Intuitive seeing will certainly add depth and meaning – wholeness – to the word, to that which has been previously uncovered through reasoned interpretation.

This Christ impulse of Spirit brought to the world inclusive love... inclusivity – rather than separation, division, fragmentation – being a necessary quality for creating wholeness within humanity, for an authentic embracing of a life of the whole perspective, and for an authentic "Yes" to the mother's command – *Work for all the children, all my children in the world.*

Shifts, true developmental shifts, call upon both mind and heart. We have talked a bit about the mind, the shift in mind that eventually brings about "thinking in a new way"... the shift from the reasoning mind of existence – anchored in existence-based philosophy – to the processing community mind of essence, anchored in the essence-based living philosophy of potential... the mind looking to the intuition of wholeness and reflective dialoging to access the wisdom of intent... to see and understand intent and intended ways of working of life in the context of now, in the context of the emerging reality of the children.

Perhaps a few thoughts regarding the heart would engender some useful seeing and dialoguing. The more common experience of the way of the heart is the response of the heart, within-the-heart to that which enters from without... often generating within fairly deep feelings – feelings of joy, of sadness, of love, etc. The perhaps less common, but that which is now called for, is a through-the-heart love, an entering of love through the heart – a heart open to the inclusive love of Christ, thus flowing from within to without... the open heart being the forgiving heart, a forgiving heart that comes not so much from the existence realities, but much more from a higher, understanding sense of our humanness... not so much focused on human failings, human weaknesses, but rather the ways of working of philosophy, perspective and particular minds – their effect on the paths we have taken and what has unfolded along those paths. It is natural, as the critical clarity of conscience illuminates what has been at work, to have some angst, some anger, perhaps desires for vengeance, etc.; none of which – if surrendered to – will advance our humanness. Now we know from experience that we can take the energies of anger and transform them into a positive forward thrust. But even that is insufficient. What is needed now, what is possible now through love entering, is genuine forgiveness – perhaps of the nature Christ expressed towards the end of his life: *Father forgive them, for they know not what they do* (Lk23:34)... a forgiveness that transcends the attachment we have to our segmented identity... a forgiveness that starts with oneness and wholeness... a forgiving heart and an intentional mind working to bring about intentional ways... ways of hope, hope for all my children in the world... intentional ways that demand faith, true faith in life... in the Life.

Our Choice

As living human beings we are both genetically and cultur-
ally encoded…

Genetic Encoding. As living human beings we, like other
species, have within, the patterns and processes of genetic
encoding – messaging inherent within life, within life's
processes of reproducing, adapting, mutating, surviving, and
so on… patterns and messaging that themselves seem to be
organized around existence – maintaining existence, ongoing existence, and including the adapting and evolving
made necessary by the dynamic nature, the changing
dynamics and forward thrust of life. Common within these
processes, perhaps more so in some than others, is the character of randomness, a randomness that both drives and
enables uniqueness… the nature of uniqueness we commonly experience in two children of the same biological
parents, same family, same community, etc., a uniqueness
that shows up in the reflective question, How can they be
so different? Yet, within this uniqueness, uniqueness within the one, there is a commonality of being of the same
species – the human species. Uniqueness, differentiation
and diversity are common characteristics inherent within
life, within life's processes… characteristics woven into and
seemingly essential to the ongoingness of life… imagery
which evokes within, some conscientious reflection and
questioning with regard to our current and increasingly
common practices of manipulation – artificial manipulation
– that is outside of the inherent ways and natural processes
of life… manipulation with regard to food production, med-
ical practices, and so on… conscientious questioning with
regard to the depth of understanding, wholistic understanding – is there sufficient understanding present, held within us
– to warrant such manipulations; or are we in reality "out-
driving our headlights," racing down the road without the

necessary light and vision of understanding, perhaps energized and fueled by commodity-based economic power pursuits… conscientious questioning perhaps worthy of reflective community dialoguing with regard to current pursuits, and imagery with regard to right and good pursuits, the nature of imagery accessible through the intuition of wholeness.

Cultural Encoding. Cultural encoding – messaging – speaks to us, speaks of us, speaks to and from our hearts and minds. Structurally and systemically we experience particular values, elements of status, taboos, symbols and stuff of success, etc. Culture as process – at the essence virtue of culture – is teaching, the process of teaching, a process that is innerly organized by philosophy. Culture is the means, the intentional means to develop and manifest the inner progressions – the stepwise advancements in our humanness… the realization of our potential to become fully and truly human.

We can gain an experientially grounded envisioning of the working of culture by reflecting upon the existence patterns and realities of life and their active presence in our existence-based culture… a culture which is itself both organized by and a manifestation of the reasoning mind of existence. We can see within that, the influence of managing and acquiring the necessities of life… the processes of surviving and the natural desire to move up levels of existence. And too, we can see the directional and cultural influence brought about by an aim to gain eternal life, to be lifted out of life's existence realities, to be rescued from sufferings, to enter into a space of peace, love and happiness; and within that we can see the inevitability of our eventually seeing ourselves as the source – acting in ways that reflect this seeing, acting as if we were god; that being viewed by some as the greatest sin of all.

However, we have come to understand that at this time, the particular advancement in our humanness being called for – the advancement required to return us to the path of life, to bring wholeness to humanity, and congruence with life intentions – requires we take up the work of creating – bringing into being – the active presence of a "work for all children, all my children, in the world" culture… not me, or my, or some children, but all children in the world… a culture that speaks to, speaks of and speaks from the intended wholeness and oneness of humanity… a culture that through its teaching processes would develop commitment and ableness to bring the world of our making into congruence with the living world of intent… a culture that would speak of a people who are walking in faith… faith in life, faith in intent and intended ways of working… a people who begin with wholeness – wholeness of humanity, wholeness of and with life… a people who would hold processes of segmentation, separation, divisiveness and power-over as taboos, not as authentic representations of who they are, or who they intend to be.

Within the context of our humanness and culture emerges the subject of language… a messaging process that is highly developed and uniquely so in humans. Woven into the teaching process of culture is language – particular patterns, expressions, words and meanings of words. We can see patterns and ways of communicating that have developed around particular work and processes (for example, building, farming, manufacturing, familying, gossiping, coffeeing, etc.). Thus language, the processes of language, will accompany and develop as we go forward, going forward by taking up the work. We know from experience the language patterns and processes related to the ways of the mind of essence, of intuition and the intuition of wholeness, of reflective dialoguing, have a unique character, a character quite different from the mind of existence and its reasoning processes.

Within the processes of essence and intuition, central to that, is reflective imagery. The inner working and, through dialogue, the reciprocally nourishing pattern of the seeing and understanding the imagery reveals is a language all of its own. The familiar statement, "A picture is worth a thousand words," comes to mind. Within essence and intuition, it is not so much a complete capturing of the outer, but the inner experiencing – often the awakening of spirit – a process of giving voice to intuition and courage to conscience that is the looked for potential of the process, a process which itself is made real through our entering with serious intent.

Within the workings of culture we can see that it can be an externally or intrinsically sourced process; we can be defined from without or from within, from existence or from essence patterns of intent, from existence desires or from essential truths.[5] With an understanding of the work and way of working of culture, we can consciously choose... choose our path, choose our teachings; we can choose teachings of love, teachings of hate, teachings of fear, teachings of hope, teachings of power-over, teachings of control, teachings of equality – the compassion of equality, teachings of positional status, teachings anchored in inclusive love, teachings in separation and segmentation, teachings of...

The choice truly is ours... a *real* exercise in free will.

---

5. Anderson, T.P. *Current Reality: The Loss of our Humanness... A Real Risk of Today.* www.pathofpotential.org.

Intentional grandmothering…

The particular role – a process role – for
  The particular work, at
    This particular time,
      This time of now:

The role of initiating the creating of a "work for all children in the world" culture.

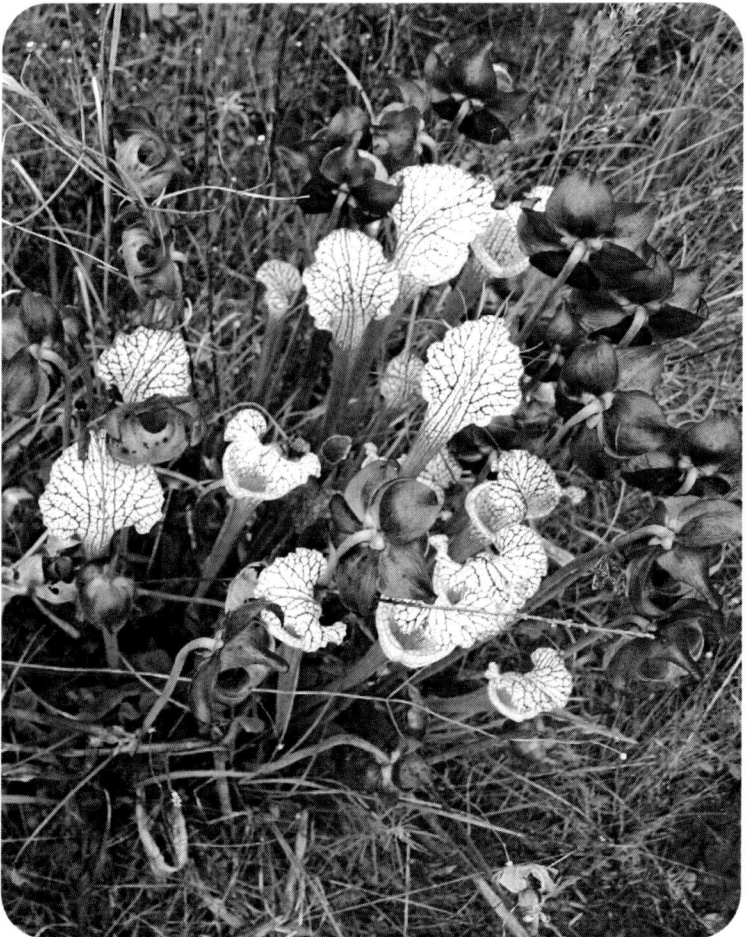

Part 2

TAKING ON AN INITIATING ROLE

The Initiating Process Role of Now

These writings on the initiating process role of now are reflections that were organized by and have emerged from a recent kitchen table gathering – an intentional dialogue – regarding the children's reality here and in the unfolding now… a gathering of those with serious intent with regard to the work of now… people willfully seeking to open the heart – to transcend, go beyond, innerly held boundaries… people willfully seeking to develop the mind – to generate within the seeing and understanding – for taking up the work, the real work before us. Real work, intentional work, is taken up, carried out through roles… the taking on of particular roles, roles having the character required for the particular work at hand… roles not so much about doing as they are about presence – a presence that emerges from willfulness and beingness.

The way of intentional dialoguing is a disciplined way, a way of managing self away from argument while simultaneously being open to the natural struggle that occurs as we experience the incongruence of that which we currently, innerly hold – hang onto, so to speak – with the emerging seeing of intent and intended ways of working. The promise and experience of this processing is that we not only see that which was not visible before, but we also increase our ableness to truly embrace – hold within – essential truths… truths essential to intended ways, to our becoming, to our moving in the direction of advancing our humanness… truths essential to our becoming more fully and truly human.

In previous reflective processing we had gained clarity with regard to the working of philosophy, the nature of philosophy required for this time of now; and a fair bit of understanding of the living philosophy of potential. And, along with this, we had come to see and understand what is the work before us:

Moving towards wholeness, away from that which divides.

Bringing the world of our making into congruence with the world of intent, intended ways.

Taking up pursuits that work for all children, all children in the world... and in particular, the creating of an active presence of a "work for all children in the world" culture... culture being the instrument and process by which we – as living human beings – advance our humanness.

And so, with a life of the whole perspective, a grasp of the work of philosophy, access to and understanding of the living philosophy of potential – the nature of philosophy now required – and clarity with regard to the work before us; the table was set, properly set for the emergence of role... the particular role, for the particular work of now. Joyfully, as the title of this book indicates, the role – *intentional grandmothering* – emerged; one cannot recall a more welcome guest at the kitchen table. This role, intentional grandmothering, brought coalescence to that which, through the intuition of wholeness, had been seen and understood... a coalescence out from which emerged a seeing of a way to go forward, to truly take up the work... to take on a role, to go into community... making real the path of our becoming an intentional people of earth.

Grandmotherly love organizes itself around the wellbeing of the children. Through intentional grandmothering, we can see the encompassing of the natural bias towards our own – our own family, our own community – and a large enough "lap" – a heart that can become truly open to all children in the world… a heart and mind that through the intuition of wholeness sees and understands that at this time the wellbeing of my own is inseparable from the wellbeing of all – all the children… the life and living of some is interwoven within the life and living of all… all of the children, the whole of life itself. And too, we can see within intentional grandmothering the willful presence of that which encompasses both the mother's command:

> *Work for all my children, all my children in the world,*

And:

> *The Father's commandment of eternal life…*
> *Eternalizing life on and through this living earth…*
> *The coming of the kingdom, of*
> *Thy will being done on this earth* (Jn12:50, Mt6:10).

All of which is only possible through the accessing and entering of the all-inclusive love that Christ – through completing his work – brought into, made accessible to earthly life… the nature of love required for the unfolding work of now… for the particular work, for the particular becoming within and among ourselves.

The going forward process is a process of will. It takes a lot of will on our part to truly open our hearts and develop the understanding required for the nature of conviction and courage the work calls for. Role clarity makes possible the taking up of the work. In the absence of role, we are reduced to doing… doing in which both beingness and willfulness are absent. It is through beingness and willfulness that love enters the process, thus the necessity for role clarity. Taking on the role of intentional grandmothering requires our developing an essence-based understanding –

an intuitive seeing – of what is at work, how we work, and where are we really – both currently and where is this path of the world of our making truly taking us… us and our children.

We have come to see intentional grandmothering as the initiating process role for taking up the work before us, the instrumental role through which the all-inclusive love Christ made accessible can truly enter into the working of our world… the living earth, our home, the home of all… the place where *Thy will is intended to be done… as it is in heaven* (Mt6:10).

An Unfolding Story of Realization...
Realizing Intended Potential

– My word will do whatever I will –

> *Thus says the Lord:*
> *Just as from the heavens*
> *   the rain and snow come down*
> *And do not return there*
> *   till they have watered the earth,*
> *   making it fertile and fruitful,*
> *Giving seed to the one who sows*
> *   and bread to the one who eats,*
> *So shall my word be*
> *   that goes forth from my mouth;*
> *It shall not return to me void,*
> *   but shall do my will,*
> *   achieving the end for which I sent it* (Is55:10-11).
> The word of the Lord.

From the beginning, will – intent, intended ways of working, intended unfolding – was actively present; *Thy will being done on this earth* (Mt6:10), this living earth, was the original and is the ongoing intent, the organizing force for that which was to unfold, for the ongoing unfolding. Will being that which was to have dominion over life, over the living earth.

It was into this willful, intentional unfolding process of life that man entered... a living creature of and from the Life... woven within the whole of life... bringing forth a uniqueness, role and work previously not present in the life processes of earth. Present within this newly arrived creature were the ableness characteristics of free will, conscience and conscious choice; inherent within was that which would free us up to honor, yet transcend – go beyond – the instinctual limitations present within all of life's creatures… an inherent potential that could, with right orientation, be exercised in accord with dominion – the will of the Source… the potential to be a willful instrument of the Source… a potential that one day could be called upon, could be realized in the unfolding process of life.

The truth of life, of our life, lies within our inner processing – inner choices, inner development, inner evolution towards becoming fully and truly human, realizing our potential within. It was the inner processing of man that led to our "leaving" the garden – an inner leaving, a shift in perspective, a moving away from intentional, intended ways… an inner leaving, not an outer departure… a choiceful process, the process of beginning our separation from the Source. A process of our moving in the direction of seeing ourselves as the source. A process of anchoring ourselves more and more to existence – the structural, the material, the energies of existence. A process of moving away from essence – patterns of intent – and away from wisdom, increasingly towards knowledge… ultimately seeking more and more capacity to manipulate life, the structuring and structures of life… seeking a world of our making that "promised" a better world than was possible previously.

Interwoven within our story of realization – interwoven in a manner similar to the way in which we are interwoven into the process of life – are ongoing interactions with the Source… some initiated by and through us; others initiated by the Source, with the Source-initiated interactions having, at times, the character of an intervention – a particular intentional impulse into life… an intervening impulse with the common aim of re-awakening and re-orienting us to intent, intended ways of the will – the dominion will of the Source. We see the presence of this as we reflect on the teachings and work of Christ. And now, in the context of the particular work and role before us, the admonishment of

Christ for each and all to *repent* (Mt4:17) – to think a new way – and the going forward prayer, *Our Father which art in heaven hallowed be Thy name*...(Mt6:9-13), he taught us, have particular significance. His admonishing us to think a new way lifts up the necessity for shifting perspectives – shifting that which organizes our thinking, determines our path and our direction. Reflecting on the prayer Christ taught us lifts up, makes visible, the intent for the kingdom – the domain of will – to come, to be actively present on this earth. And, not surprisingly, the going forward prayer holds as central that which was and is the original ongoing intent: *Thy will being done on this earth as it is in heaven.* And further we see a clear reference to our experience – most particularly our inner experience – of life. We see prayerful consideration of life's necessities, trespasses, indebtedness and temptations – in terms of forgiving and avoiding... truly a life, a here and unfolding now life-centered prayer... taught to us by he who, through demonstration and expression (Jn14:6), was *the life* – of and from the Life – and *the truth* – the truth of the ongoing, unfolding love of the Source – and *the way* – the pattern and path for realization of potential... *shall not return to me void, but rather achieving the end for which I sent it*... the nourishing way of the will. And quite naturally, received by many as "good news" was the reconnecting of ourselves to the Source, and the seeing of a path whereby the prodigal son can return – be welcomed back, forgiven and be in good standing – to the intended ways of the Source.

What gets lifted up in our reflections on the admonishings and teachings of Christ is both the usefulness of and the necessity for some essential understanding with regard to how we work, what is at work, and intended ways of working... both useful and necessary for freeing us up to take up the particular work of now... the nature of understanding that allows us to consciously and conscientiously choose our path.

Perhaps a good pausing point for this reflection is:

> Man was made for the garden...

> The garden was not made for man.

> Man was intended to have a significant role... a reciprocally nourishing instrumental role of dominion; the truth of which requires our coming from a life of the whole perspective... a perspective authentic to and of the garden of intent...

> Always remembering, of course, *if love is not present in the process, love will not be present in the outcomes.*

Some Essential Seeing and Understanding...
The Development of which requires Intentional Dialoguing

Further Thoughts on Role

As living human beings we are genetically and cul-
turally encoded.

Culture – the structuring processes of culture – can
both restrain and enable the intended advancement of our humanness.

Each and all have purpose, intentional purpose,
which is inclusive of self and family, but which
reaches beyond those to the whole of humanity,
and ultimately embraces the whole of life.

At times, like now, the taking on of intentional
purpose, intentional role, requires of us the not so
comfortable "act" of stepping outside of current
culture... reaching beyond its limitations, the
desires and affirmations – being good, being successful, etc. – of our culture. And within that culture, reaching beyond the limitations and affirmations of the culture of the various communities to
which we belong, in which we participate – for
example, academic, business, religious, scientific,
educational, political, etc.

Intentional reaching is an act of will, a process of
will requiring wholistic seeing and understanding
not present in the restraining culture; but a seeing
and understanding required for the work of now...
the work essential to intended unfolding.

We have seen these notions at work in previous reflections

on the authentic "Yes" of Mary… a yes that understood the cultural implications of her accepting – embracing – the work, the intentional, instrumental work before her. Recent reflections on the transfiguration of Christ have brought to light some similar seeing. Given the culture of the times – its pursuits, what was leading its thinking; the sense of accomplishment with regard to one's own, the validation of those that had come before; and the ultimate stamp of approval from the Father – no doubt Christ could, in a celebratory way, have accepted the acclaim and inclinations of his people. Yet, he, with great resolve, went forth along a path not visible within the culture… a path of realization – the realization of potential, the realization of intent… a path of bringing – making accessible on earth to earth's people – an all-inclusive love… a path of manifesting spirit through the completion of his work… a path of reconciling forgiveness, that through the sending of the Spirit – Spirit accessible to all – would make possible our taking up the work… work that could bring forth that which *was greater than he himself had performed* (Jn14:12) – the visible miracles so necessary and satisfying to the reasoning mind of existence, the dominant mind of that time, of our time. And ultimately he made visible a path, *a way* (Jn14:6) for us to follow… a path not of our making; rather a path of intent, of intended ways… a new path, yet the original path.

It is this notion of *way* that is so revealing at this time. *I am the way* (versus I am it) is about process. It is about seeing, enabling and understanding process… ongoing, unfolding process… and ultimately seeing life as process, seeing truth as process, seeing Christ as process… process organized by the particular work of now and carried out through roles – initiating roles; the particular initiating role of now being *intentional grandmothering*.

In contemplating and dialoguing this role – intentional grandmothering – it is important to hold in mind two critical anchors, anchors that serve as both ground and guiding star, those being compassion, the compassion of equality, and intuition, the intuition of wholeness. It is through the compassion of equality that we stay connected to the Source… thus the need to work for all children, all my children in the world. It is through the intuition of wholeness that we stay connected to – see and understand – intent and intended ways of working. Through the intuition of wholeness we gain access to the wisdom of intent… wisdom being present to the unfolding creation. Thus the instrumentality of the intuition of wholeness in the work of bringing the world of our making into congruence with the world of intent… and further, wholeness is not only the ongoing aim of intuition, but is also the aim of the work of now… an aim expressed as moving towards wholeness, away from that which divides.

With regard to taking up our work and role, three processes have emerged as central – intentional writing, intentional reading, and intentional dialoguing – each of which has been described in previous writings. Recently, however, we have begun to see intentional dialoguing as a true reconcile – that which embraces, lifts up, makes more whole and complete that which was revealed in intentional writing and reading… a seeing that has been an experiential reality for those who have been actively present in the dialogue.

Reflecting further on the experience of the dialogue participants brings forth these thoughts. Mind is process, having much more of a being character than the character of function – function having the nature of character more associated with the structure we call the brain, and the functioning more related to thinking, problem solving, etc. Mind in process creates an energy field which enables and elevates the process and processing; not unlike that which we witness when a returning bee engages the hive in the ritual dance regarding a newly discovered field of flowers, clover, etc. Here again, right nature of processing generates a particular mind within which an "eye" emerges that can see what was previously unseen… especially in terms of work and role. All of which brings added insight to the unfolding understanding that at this time, community is the smallest whole.

Shifts, true shifts – that which reaches beyond incremental improvements of what is – call upon, require of us an advancement in humanness… require our moving in the direction of becoming more fully, more truly, more wholly human. The taking up of the way and path, the teachings, the work and the all-inclusive love of Christ, makes this seeable and possible. Shifts, true shifts begin with and look to process – the initiating source of spirit and energy; that which sustains the potential in an activity… our potential to be and become, at this time of now, an intentional people of earth.

Role, by its nature, looks to process – the seeing, the leading, the managing of process – and when done intuitively, seeks wholeness… wholeness more akin to realizing potential than solving a problem… moving more in the direction of increasing ableness – ableness to be and become. As role shifts in accord with the shift and work of now, the seeing process and seeking wholeness of intuition are not diminished but rather become an entry point, experiential ground and ableness, for reaching beyond self and family to the whole of humanity; and ultimately embracing the whole of life… the depth and wholeness required of an intentional role… the depth and wholeness clearly present in the role of intentional grandmothering… a role grounded in the compassion of equality and one that develops, accesses and comes from the intuition of wholeness – that which enables us to see intent and intended ways of working. For development, added ableness, seeing and understanding with regard to the intuition of wholeness, we look to the three processes of intentional reading, writing and dialoguing... which in accord are inspirited and energized by prayerful questioning – seeking to see intended ways – and an active and growing presence of serious intent – intent to take up the work, take on an intentional role.

As we have contemplated and dialogued the work now before us and as the image of intentional grandmothering has emerged, so too has emerged the aim of creating an active presence of a "work for all children in the world" culture. Creating an active presence – perhaps not unlike that which Christ lifted up through saying, *Where two or more are gathered together in my name, there am I in their midst* (Mt18:20), versus changing, constructing, putting in place, etc. – shifts our focus away from doing, away from problem solving, and moves us towards role... towards being and becoming... increasing our ableness to come from, to hold in mind, and bring forth in process, true consideration of all my children in the world, true consideration of the whole of life... processes more akin to reconciling than compromising, more aimed at advancing humanness than incremental improvements. All of which brings to mind leading, planning and managing – essential and common processes of humankind; now, however, seeking to see them not only in the context of our role, but also within community – the smallest whole of our time, this time of now.

In contemplating and dialoguing the processes of leading, planning and managing, it is critical that we remember the imagery and work of *an active presence* versus the common inclinations of predetermine, make happen, etc.; also remembering that all roles seek to serve the intended unfolding of this time… an intended unfolding emerging from and towards an image held by the Source – not directed by our image, our will; rather *Thy will being done* (Mt6:10). Remembering and honoring this does not absolve us from development and preparation; but does add clarity to the way and work of our role. In that regard some thoughts about leading, planning and managing have emerged.

> Central to intentional leading is that which will *work for all my children in the world*… remembering that all children are children of and from life and totally dependent upon the vitality and viability of the life processes of earth.

> Central to intentional planning is *the Father's commandment is eternal life* (Jn12:50) – eternalizing life on and through this earth… remembering that our ways of living and working are intended to be harmonious and congruent with intent and intended ways. This is both the original intent and the everlasting intent.

> Central to intentional managing is that we *come from above, not from below*… that our processes are sourced in essence patterns of intent versus existence – the needs and desires of existence… remembering that it is through work – real work – that spirit is accessed and manifested… work and role being the means by which essence is manifested in existence.

And, of course central to all of this is the often stated truth: *If love is not present in the process, love will not be present in the outcomes.* If love, all-inclusive love, does not enter the process, the particular advancement of humanness required for the intended shift will not occur; without all-inclusive love, it will be impossible. If all-inclusive love is to enter, truly enter, it is necessary that we:

Pursue reaching beyond self and family; including the whole of humanity, the whole of life.

Engage in processes that are more fully embracing of the whole of the truth of Christ; processes inclusive of salvation and of returning; but reaching beyond, embracing becoming, the coming of the kingdom.

Embrace the whole of the truth of Life – the Source of life, of intended ways of working of life on this earth. Seek seeing and understanding; move away from manipulative knowledge and ways.

It is through serious intent and willful pursuit of the necessary that we engage in the process of creating receptive instruments and pathways for all-inclusive love to enter into our ways such that the intended advancement in humanness – that which is required for continued unfolding – can be brought about.

Perhaps this is a useful stopping point for this writing... writing that is evoking in me some imagery of a command: *Be ye like children* (Mt18:3)... and seeing this while remembering that the purposeful work of the children is to make life whole.

Then... and Now

In seeking to add imagery and understanding to the initiating role of intentional grandmothering, we find ourselves reflecting on then and now. "Then" being thought of as the time of Christ's presence on earth, and the early days (the first two to three hundred years) of Christianity; "now" being considered as the immediate now, the stirring, the work and role before us now... now, at this time of potential.

Taking on a role, an initiating role, is not a foreign process for women... not then; not now. Looking back, we can readily see this in the authentic "Yes" of Mary... the yes through which Christ entered into the world; and further in her active presence in the initiating of the work of Christ. We can also see this in the unfolding process of the risen Christ, not only in Mary Magdalene and the women who first embraced the risen Christ, but ongoingly in the early and unfolding days of Christianity... and is visibly present today. Reflecting on this through the eyes and understanding of intuition, we begin to see:

THEN: Here the women, through intuition – seeing process, seeking wholeness – saw the process of Christ and within that, the potential wholeness of self, of family, of humanity. Through the compassion of caring for – caring for the poor, the sick, the outcasts, etc. – they sustained their and our connectedness with the Source; and through that could innerly experience a oneness with the Source, with the Love of the Source, with the Hope within the Source... a compassion expressed through good works of charity, works not aimed at gaining salvation, but rather meaningful ways for following the path of Christ... ways for enabling love – advancing humanness love – to enter into our world, to enter into our ways of living and working... an

78

advancement of humanness now possible through the reconciling forgiveness brought about through the work of Christ. They looked to the teachings/gospels of Christ for seeing and understanding intent... paying heed to the reasoned interpretation of these brought forth by the reasoning mind of existence – the dominant mind of the time; yet (a significant "yet" given the work of now) wisely did not surrender the powers of intuition – powers essential to leading and organizing the "kitchen table process" of that time, powers essential for processes within family and community. Thus the gift, the necessary instrument for advancing our humanness, for moving towards wholeness, and becoming more fully and truly human, was kept alive... alive and accessible for the work of today.

NOW: At this time there is yet again an intuitive stirring... a restless awakening that is being innerly experienced by more and more of us... a shift, a true and real advancement of our humanness, is seeking to come about. Now, women are being called to extend, develop and realize the potential of this gift of intuition... to do so through accessing and developing the intuition of wholeness – the seeing of process, of intent, of the intended ways of working of life; seeking wholeness within and through life... and seeing and seeking the wholeness of the truth of Christ... being called not only to see life as process, but also to see Christ as process... to see Christ as the manifesting will of the Source; to see Christ in terms of the *coming of the kingdom*, and in terms of *Thy will being done on this earth* (Mt6:10) – in the here and unfolding now.

> A call not so much about returning, but rather a clear focus on becoming, on our becoming an intentional people of earth... a people preparing the way for the *coming of the kingdom*.

A call for establishing an intended, realizable at this time, connection to the Source… connecting to the Source through the compassion of equality, the nature of compassion expressed in working for all my children in the world… the nature of work and ways of working that are bringing and will continue to bring into and within our communities, ever increasing depth and meaning to the commandments of *Love God; Love one another as I have loved you* (Mk12:30, Jn13:34)… which, following the pattern of truth, will bring increasing oneness and wholeness as well. For it is the way of truth to enfold the truths of the previous into the intended unfolding; having them emerge with greater depth, meaning and wholeness… more complete expressions of essence.

A call requiring a life of the whole perspective of the teachings and gospels of Christ… a necessary perspective for seeing the whole of the truth of Christ; the wholeness of the intent of Christ… the wholeness of the intent of Christ lifted up as he taught us to pray:

Our Father in heaven, hallowed be Thy name.
Thy kingdom come, Thy will be done, on earth as in heaven…

Reflecting on what has been written, with particular attention to what is now being called for, brings to mind the necessity for accessing, utilizing and developing the intuitive mind of essence. It is through intuition that it becomes possible to answer "Yes" to this call… an initiating yes, carried out through the role of intentional grandmothering… a yes that draws upon both heart and mind… draws upon both the openness to Spirit and the manifesting of spirit. This reflecting also brings forth some imagery…

> *Seeing lamps* (Mt25:1-13), *lamps of serious intent, at*
> *the ready;*
> *with oil, the oil of intuition, in ample supply…*
> *The hearing of approaching footsteps along the path…*
> *an excited anticipation of the coming…*
> *an approaching realization of the reality and urgency of*
> *NOW…*

Perhaps a good place to pause.

Now Needed

Coming from Above... or Coming from Below

Coming from above...
> Or coming from below

Coming from Thy will being done...
> Or acting from my will, my wish

Coming from essence...
> Or coming from existence

Being innerly, intuitively, organized...
> Or externally, existentially, determined.

The inner stirring that more and more of us are experiencing, and gaining clarity of through the intentional processes of reading, writing and dialoguing, is awakening within an aspiration to come from above – commonly starting within self, but also seeing it as a necessity for ourselves as community, and as a people of earth. An aspiration that becomes more real, more personally held, through the presence and development of serious intent; serious intent being that which comes about, enters within us as we see and understand the situation before us as being truly – undeniably, no longer ignorable – serious... and in the context of the reality of today, truly serious with regard to the children – all the children – and with regard to life – the whole of life. And too, we know from experience, the necessity for having serious intent with regard to the work before us. In the absence of serious intent, the will, the willful effort to develop the seeing and understanding the work requires, is neither present, nor accessible. And we also know from experience that having serious intent increases our ableness to access spirit and bring conscientiousness and conscious choice to that which we pursue… ensuring that, that which we pursue is truly anchored in coming from above, not sourced in my will, my wishes.

Coming from above – pursuing our becoming aspiration – requires, at this time, a life of the whole perspective, a perspective that fully embraces our humanness, our human potential, through the encompassing of the truths of our livingness… of our being intentionally, not accidentally, members in the larger community of life… people of earth, the living earth, of and from life; from the Life. To separate ourselves from life, from the intended ways of working of life; is to separate ourselves from the Source; it is the way of moving in the direction of my will versus *Thy will being done on this earth* (Jn12:50, Mt6:10)… the way that inevitably leads to our believing, acting from and as if, we are the source… as if we are the source of hope, of a better life, of an existence free of discomfort. And thus free to shape – conforming with our wishes, our image, our will – the unfolding of life on this earth, and within that to bring forth a structuring, existence-based culture… a culture organized around the materials and energies of existence, one that is free from essence patterns of intent… a culture that looks to the reasoning mind of existence, to reasoned interpretation, for direction and answers – the "hows" and "whats" of daily life.

Mind is such a part of us… of our humanness, of our ways of seeing, thinking and doing… of developing our world view, of how we see and engage our world, the world, and how we go about things… how we bring forth that which we require to sustain ourselves, and to advance our ways of working and living. Mind as process is directionally organizing… it provides the means for the living out of our philosophy… and it is the means by which we advance our humanness.

The particular mind, for the particular advancement in

humanness being called for, is the intuitive mind of essence... a mind that builds on the capacity – seeing process, seeking wholeness – of intuition... the previously developed capacities of intuition. Intuition, through the intuitive mind of essence, is wholistically extended and developed to see wholeness in the context of the whole of life... to take on a life of the whole perspective... to see and understand intent and intended ways of working of life. It is this seeing, the seeing that emerges from the development of the eye of the intuitive mind of essence, that creates within us an experience quite different from thinking – the analytical nature of process we experience through the reasoning mind of existence... an experience unique and different enough that some have described it as not thinking or not having to think... which at times creates frustration both within intuition, and within reason. The seeing, the literal seeing, imaging process of intuition is a bit of a mystery to the reasoning mind of existence – an "uncontrollable, irrational process" versus the methodical, step by step, procedure of reason. Intuition being a seeing and imaging process that creates within a depth of conviction and confirmation – truth – that does not lend itself, nor require, the fact generating, proof seeking methodology of reason. However, once seen it can provide guidance to the structuring, existence-based processes of reason... that which is directionally organized by the reasoning mind of existence.

Returning a bit to coming from above or coming from below, we can contrast and perhaps better see the work and role of each: the reasoning mind of existence, the intuitive mind of essence. The reasoning mind of existence comes from, operates within existence – the visible, the factual, the provable... and follows an analytical path of reductionism – smaller and smaller parts, more and more elements, highly specific differentiations, be they between elements, roles, laws, etc. A nature of processing once described by a teacher of mine as "learning more and more about less and less" – a somewhat humorous, but insightful imagery. These patterns, given the dominance of the reasoning mind of existence, are present throughout... readily seeable in such fields as religion-theology, science-engineering, society-policy, etc. A coming from existence pattern that is anchored in existence-based philosophies... all of which through time and reductionism, naturally diminish our seeing, accessing and seeking of wholeness... wholeness of intent, wholeness with regard to intended ways of working of life, wholeness of self, community, etc.

To be sure, the aim of contrasting the reasoning mind of existence and the intuitive mind of essence is not about dominance, but rather seeing the necessity – the work and role, and the potential – that lies within both, seeing them in the context of coming from above, and the work of now. The particular work of now aimed at bringing the world of our making into congruence with the world of intent is perhaps the most vivid example of the uniqueness and role of both. Serious intent with regard to congruence requires both the wholeness – the intentional seeing of the intuitive mind of essence – and the structuring – the analytical processing capacity of the reasoning mind of existence. Reflecting on the essential process of coming from above – bringing essence into existence through spirit manifesting work – provides added imagery to the complementarity of the work and roles of the uniquely different minds.

Complementarity – true complementarity – requires the active, authentic presence, a reciprocally nourishing equality, of both minds... a recognizing of the significance and value of each with regard to the work before us. And too, we have experienced and can see the limitations and hazards of dominance – the dominance of the one to the exclusion of the other. We only have to reflect upon the era of the dominance of the reasoning mind of existence and the inevitable realities of today to see the consequences of dominance; the realities and consequences that have emerged in the absence of wholeness – the intentional wholeness of intuition, the intuitive mind of essence... consequences and realities with regard to the children, with regard to the whole of life... consequences and realities that lift up the limitations of reason, of reason unguided by the wisdom of intent... consequences and realities that have emerged from seeking manipulative knowledge versus congruence with the intended ways of working of life... consequences and realities that reflect the reductionism patterns and lack of completeness and wholeness brought about through insulated – free of essence – reasoning and reasoned interpretations, not just in the material and energy fields of science-engineering, but also within the fields of religion-theology, and society-policy as well.

All of which brings us back to intentional grandmothering: The particular role, a process role, for the particular work at this particular time, this time of now... a time, a role, and a process that requires the directional organizing of the intuitive mind of essence... directional organizing brought about not through expertise, or our becoming experts; but rather through the seeing and understanding made visible through the eye of the intuitive mind of essence.

Creating an Active Presence... Living out the Intentional Role

Going forth into community, we enter interactions with a stead-
fast resolve – with courage and conviction... a resolve made pos-
sible through a life of the whole perspective and through our being
innerly, intuitively organized... such that the presence we create,
the thoughts we lift up, are a reflection of essence – essence pat-
terns of intent... patterns of intent with regard to the unfolding
process of now...

A life of the whole perspective that through the living philosophy of potential embraces the truths of returning and
makes visible the truths of becoming – the necessary and
realizable potential for our becoming fully, truly and wholly
human... a living philosophy working to make visible the
path of intent – the here and unfolding now path of intent
– and the work and role(s) the particular advancement in
our humanness being called for requires...

A life of the whole perspective – made practical and practice-able through the living philosophy of potential... a
perspective that brings reconciling wholeness and meaning
to the visible, the intuitively obvious, and to the invisible... a perspective that brings the seeing and understanding that, through the accessing of the intuition of wholeness, becomes real and practice-able...

A life of the whole perspective that makes possible the
potential for wholeness within – within self, within the
whole of humanity, within the whole of life – and a oneness
with the Source – the Source of life, the Life... a potential
wholeness and oneness that requires of us the seeing of life
as process, the seeing of Christ as process – embracing fully
the truth of Christ lifted up in his process depiction of himself, of his work: *I am the way, and the truth, and the life...*
He who goes to the Father comes through me (Jn14:6)...

A resolve energized by the intuitively obvious, that which requires neither proof, nor energies expended in argument or the development of rationalizations; but rather thoughtfully accepts that which is inherently obvious – whole and complete – within itself, the reflectively intuitively obvious, such as:

There is a Source; we are not the source;

There is intent and intended ways of working within life;

All of life – ourselves, our children included – depends upon nourishing, life giving waters, and breathable, inspiriting air;

There is hazard, serious hazard to each and all, in political boundaries that work to inhibit and diminish, rather than enhance and vitalize the working of essential life processes...

A resolve that intuitively sees the limitations and destiny of current ways and current path... ways and path of diminishing humanness, of diminishing vitality and viability of life's processes, of life itself... and through that, an increasingly hopeless reality for the children, all my children in the world...

A resolve that is conscious of the ways and working of culture... and alert to the particular patterns and practices of our current existence-based culture. A resolve that sees and experiences the seductive processes of reason – reason unguided by wisdom – that are present and active within our existence-based culture, within its demands for proof as evidence of truth... a process of reductionism that inevitably obscures and inhibits the embracement of that which only exists wholistically. A resolve that sees and understands these reasoned responses are naturally present in the structuring response of a culture... a culture which seeks to sustain the current – current ways, current pursuits... a culture seeking to sustain ways and pursuits uninhibited by wisdom – the wisdom of intent – and thus seeking to restrain that which needs to, is intentionally seeking to unfold: the shift, the advance in our humanness required at this time... a culture which ultimately seeks to maintain our being externally – existentially – determined...

A resolve inspired by faith – faith in intent and intended ways... faith in the way of truth: the truths of the previous unfolding are enfolded within the intended unfolding and emerge as deeper, more wholistic expressions of truth. Thus truths, truths currently held in "my faith," are not lost, but rather enriched, more fully realize-able through seeing life as process, seeing Christ as process – not unlike the experience of "then" – with the truths made visible through the seeing of the process of Christ becoming more wholistic, a deeper expression of the essence present within the previous...

A resolve further inspired by the whole of the truth of Christ... a truth that embraces both returning and becoming... the *coming of the kingdom*, the intention of the Source for *Thy will being done on this earth* (Mt6:10).

All of which brings us back to work and role... the particular role, the initiating role of the intentional unfolding process of now... the process of work to bring about the particular advancement of humanness made possible through the all-inclusive love of Christ... the particular upward shift of intent... a manifestation of the expectations of the Source... expectations expressed through the word and through the works – the intentional ways and unfolding of the living creation...

Thus, we see more clearly now, this role: The initiating process role of intentional grandmothering is not a role that entertains doubt, doubtfulness, fearfulness; but rather clarity of conviction, courage of conscience… a role requiring receptive hearts – hearts receptive to the stirring, the intuitive stirring of Spirit, the awakening of serious intent… a role, given the work of now, requiring intuitively receptive hearts, and the development of the intuitive mind of essence.

It is through seeing Christ as process and
seeing life as process that Christ becomes
intuitively present within life…
within the whole of life… within our life…
within the ongoing intended unfolding of life.

Part 3

SERIOUSLY PURSUING THE WAY OF INTENT REQUIRES SEEING CHRIST AS PROCESS…
Only Possible through taking a Life of the Whole Perspective

The Essential Petition

Father, I glorified you on earth by accomplishing the work that you gave me to do (Jn17:4).

We, each and all have work, work and roles given us, our part in the work of eternalizing life on earth, our part which calls for our becoming reciprocally nourishing within the whole of life… work which begins with opening hearts… at this time of now begins with taking up pursuits that work for all children in the world, creating an active presence of a "work for all children in the world" culture; bringing to mind the community Prayer to the Father (Mt6:9-13, translated from Greek)…

Father of us;
Father in Heaven…

Let be made whole the name of you,
Let come the kingdom of you,
Let be done the will of you…

> *as in Heaven, also on the earth.*

The daily bread of us, give to us today…
And forgive us the debts of us, as also we forgive the debtors
of us…
And lead us not into temptation, but deliver us from evil.

Because of you is the kingdom, and the power, and the glory
to the ages.

Amen.

The word, *let*, stands out:

Let be made whole the name of you,
Let come the kingdom of you,
Let be done the will of you…

The prayer is the full recognition that all that is truly desirable for the people of earth calls for the Father ongoingly "letting" this unfold… the Father ongoingly willing, the will of the Father being ongoing process. Jesus reopened the pathway, reopened our relatedness to the Father of us; the Father must let happen that for which we are praying… the continuing intent of the Father… the eternal upwardly unfolding life. The Father of us has all power. Which brings us to the truth, anything of significance – *any glory to the ages* – is through the Father; as lifted up by Jesus early in his teaching years, *whoever lives the truth comes to the light, so that his works may be clearly seen as done in God* (Jn3:21).

The Prayer to the Father is a petition, a prayer of petition, the petition looked for from us, a petition not for our eternal life in heaven, but for the kingdom of the Father to come to the earth, the petition asking the Father of us to use his power to let us *make whole his name*, let us take up our role in *Thy kingdom coming*, let us take up the work of *Thy will being done…. on this earth…* as intended.

We can understand the essentiality of this petition, for there is much that we require to be able to accomplish the work we petition the Father give us…

The ever-flowing will of our Father.

Access to wisdom, the wisdom of intent… access to seeing the intent of the Father, and the Father's intended ways of working of life.

A way to accomplish this work we are given… the way

of intentionality.

But what stands out here is that, for our making whole, doing, taking up work, embracing roles, the Father of us must *let*... the Father must will that we take a role in *eternalizing life on earth as in heaven* (Jn12:50; Mt6:10)... an ongoing willing with hazard. For his gift of wisdom from/through the Spirit of truth, is pure gift – pure gift of love. And it would seem, he is not seeing from us at the present time, the collective capacity to live in keeping with the pattern of the process provided by his Son. Yes, unique individuals have and do selflessly sacrifice their lives in the service of others, but are we – humanity – moving towards or away from becoming one people, one humanity; towards or away from wholeness, towards or away from becoming instruments of all-inclusive love? And, as a friend so generously shared, when the wisdom of intent is given by the Spirit, the temptation is great to take self as source and use such for my will, not Thy will.

Reflecting on the three petitions for that which was originally intended to be brought into being on this earth – making whole the name, kingdom coming, will being done – we notice the significance of the ending of the prayer, *because of you is the kingdom, and the power, and the glory to the ages.* Because of the Father of us, and only because of the Father, will there be his kingdom on the earth; the will of him – *eternal life* – on the earth; and the glory of him – *the accomplishing of the work he gives us to do* – on this earth... to every age. No age truly advances without *because of him*, without *Thy will*. The Father of life is the Life; the Father is Life.

Looking to the second part of the prayer, the first part having revealed the purpose for which our lives, life itself exists; the second part revealing what help we need in taking up and staying on the path, and avoiding the hazards and "landmines" along the way…

Daily bread, every day… food for our hearts and minds… most of all, the food of our called work, the food of love – all-inclusive love – and the food of wisdom – the wisdom of intent and intended ways of working of life – to carry out our called work. Reminding us of Jesus' words, *My food is to do the will of the one who sent me and to accomplish his work* (Jn4:34). Our food is to do the will of the Father, the Source of all and to accomplish his work.

Debt forgiveness. As we take up our intended work, we may be neither efficient nor necessarily effective. We may clumsily extract from, more than we nourish the ongoing life on this earth. Forgive us this debt to life which we may build up as we, in community, take up our part in this work, our role, our purpose in *eternalizing life on earth as in heaven.* Forgive us this debt to life, this debt to the Life. Forgive us our debt to the future life of all children… particularly debt which threatens the ongoingness of life itself. Forgive us our debt to *the Father whose command is life everlasting… on earth as in heaven* (Jn12:50).

Lead us not into temptation – the temptation (all the way back to the garden) to take ourselves as the source – source of love, wisdom, etc.; keep us out of temptation to take ourselves as source of life. Please, Lord, give us enough wisdom to accomplish our work/the work you give us, but no more than we need… hence daily… give us daily what we need… do not waste or risk more on us: *Lead us not into temptation.*

But deliver us from evil… deliver us from all that moves us away from life – deliver us from all that moves us away from the wholeness and fullness and light of life – and towards death… deliver us from divisiveness, from all that moves us, as humanity, away from being reciprocally nourishing within the whole of life. Deliver us from a world of our making that leads all life on earth, including human life, towards death.

What becomes visible is the one thing we say we are doing, will do: ...*as also we forgive the debtors of us*. This is the only thing we say we will do... ongoingly. This must be the essential thing, the underpinning of all else, that which calls for as well as leads to our becoming meek and humble of heart (*Blessed the meek communities; for they shall inherit the earth* (Mt5:5)). Letting go of self-aggrandizement, letting go of self above others, letting go of self as source, and becoming an open forgiving *community* heart (recall that the Lord's Prayer to the Father is from *"we"*), is essential to our inheriting earth, inheriting from the Father, the work of eternalizing life on this earth... at this time, that beginning with the "work for all children in the world" work. Without forgiveness, without becoming open forgiving community hearts, there is no void – no receptive instrument – into which the all-inclusive love of Christ can enter; we risk thinking of ourselves as "owning" earth, thinking ourselves as hierarchical to one another; we risk turning our backs to our intended work and role in *eternalizing life, as in heaven, also on the earth*. An echo, it seems, of the commandment, *Love one another as I have loved you* (Jn13:34). And we have enough of a grasp of the pattern of that process – the pattern of all-inclusive love – to see the intentional work we have before us, the change essential, for living daily that commandment... and we now see a bit more clearly, the essentiality of living from and to this *new commandment* given us by Christ, if we – humanity – are ever to have the ableness to ongoingly – *to the end of the age* – take up our intended work and role in the *Father's commandment – eternal life* (Jn12:50) – which the Prayer to the Father reveals is intended *on earth as in heaven*.

We are beginning to get an image of the here and now, on this earth, working of the commandment, *Love God* (Mk12:30). Bringing us back to the first petitioning words of the prayer: *Let be made whole the name of you... the name of you...* that name being *I AM* (Ex3:14; Jn14:6):

I AM

I AM... the Life;

> *Your work is to make Life real... on this earth at this time.*

> *There is no other way;*

> *There is no other truth;*

> *There is no other Life.*

I AM WHO AM.

Following the Way of Intent
Reflections emerging from Ongoing Dialogue

Following the Way of Intent: 1

The Son of Man has nowhere to rest his head… Follow me… Let the dead bury their dead. I am… the life (Lk9:58-60; Jn14:6).

Life enters… life enters at the beginning of life… and rests not until the last day. This is true of the Life. Life – the will force which sustains the livingness of the human person, the livingness of all creatures of earth, the livingness of earth – *never rests his head.*

The dead, those without faith in Life, those who do not see and become instruments of all-inclusive love – the compassion of caring about – are already dead; they are not participating in life, in the *coming of the kingdom…*

Follow me… follow the Life, follow the process of Christ, follow the pattern of the process of Christ, follow the essence virtue of Christ… follow the way of all-inclusive love, of inclusivity – life of the all, life of the whole. Become instruments of all-inclusive love by becoming forgiving community hearts… becoming open community that comes from a life of the whole perspective, community that works for all children – all children in the world – community on the path of becoming reciprocally nourishing within the whole of life… building community soul, manifesting community spirit… in the way of Christ – no looking back to the world left behind.

Follow me… you too will have nowhere to rest your head. The kingdom of heaven is not a place but a process… the process taking direction from the mothers' command, *Work for all my children in the world...* never ending work, work possible through becoming open forgiving community hearts... community hearts open to all-inclusive love; work possible through our embracing the truth of our membership in the whole of life... *life from Life.*

Following the Way of Intent: 2

The harvest is abundant but the laborers are few... Go on your way; behold, I am sending you like lambs to the wolves... Into whatever house you enter, first say, Peace to this household. If a peaceful person lives there, your peace will rest on him; but if not, it will return to you (Lk10:2-6).

Only through developing the mind of essence, the community mind receptive to wisdom, wisdom of the Source, the intent of the Source and the intended way of working of life, are we able to see – to see our work and role. Seeing our work and role, we are able to use the reasoning mind of existence as a means for carrying out our work. Yet, when the mind of existence uses reason to control life, to make the world of existence superordinate to the intent of the Source, there is no peace... *no peace in the household*, no peace in the community. The world of existence does not warmly welcome the world of essence, hence the image, *like lambs to the wolves*.

The harvest is abundant, but the laborers few. When Life enters – at the beginning of life – the essence pattern of intent enters, essence pattern being the virtue enfolded within life by the Source... virtue intended to be unfolded within humankind through our becoming reciprocally nourishing within the whole of life, through our participating in and co-operating with the unfolding of this essential potential – the essence virtue – within each and within all, within the whole of life... all calling for reason being led by the mind of essence – the essence mind being our process mind, the community mind which, when open and receptive, sees and hears the intent of the Source and intended ways of working of life. *The harvest is abundant* – essential virtue imbedded within, intent and intended ways of working imbedded within – *and the laborers few* – few quieting

103

ourselves, few communities coming together in reflective intentional dialogue, ongoingly building the essence mind, the mind essential to and enabling our participating in the harvest... few communities taking up our part in eternalizing life, taking up our work and role in *Thy kingdom coming, Thy will being done on this earth* (Mt6:10) at this time... taking up our community part in *the eternalizing life command of the Source* (Jn12:50). Leading to asking ourselves: Through our time on earth, what is our time on earth returning to life? What is our time on earth returning to the Source, returning to the Life, returning to the ongoingness of life? Worry not about your place in heaven; worry about your intended work – your intentional purpose here on earth. Participating in the harvest being the taking up of work and the embracing of role and entering the process – the process of life, the process of Christ.

I give you praise, Father, Lord of heaven and earth, for although you have hidden these things from the wise and learned you have revealed them to the childlike (Lk10:21).

The mind of existence does not "see" the whole; the mind of existence divides... is partial... problem solves existence. The reasoning mind of existence views as real only that which can be revealed through the senses. Essence is *hidden from the wise and learned*... from those who see life in terms of the structures it enters, the structures it makes... not as spirit entering. Essence, the essence pattern – the pattern of essential virtues imbedded in life – is hidden. Essential virtues are "seeable," are *revealed to the childlike*. The Father reveals intent only to the childlike... to those who believe in life, believe in life's mysteries, believe there is another world beyond the existence world, that being the world of essence, the world of intent... the childlike believe in the intent of the Father... believe they can "hear" the voice of the Spirit – hear intent – and "see" patterns of intent – intended ways of working of life, ways that unfold the potential hidden within. The childlike are open and receptive to the wisdom of Spirit entering. The childlike are on a path of moving towards wholeness, away from the divisiveness of the existence mind... and by so doing, are on the path of becoming one with the Source... and manifesting spirit – making the processing of the essence virtues of life available forever and to all on earth... taking their part in eternalizing life on the earth.

Hiding intent from the wise and learned being praiseworthy. For being wise and learned in the absence of having faith in Life, in the Spirit of life, hazards the seeing and understanding of intent and intended ways of working (wisdom gifts of the Spirit) being used for my will, my wishes, our own;

rather than for community fulfilling *Thy will on this earth* (Mt6:10)... as intended.

Whoever is not against us is for us (Lk9:50). He who is not divided and divisive... he who is not leading thinking, not starting from the mind of existence – the mind of segmentation, of separation – is with us... is coming from, wishing to come from, or working with us to start our thinking from the intuitive mind of essence, the mind of seeing potential hidden within... potential imbedded when life entered... the community mind essential to unfolding potential, as intended.

Following the Way of Intent: 4

The kingdom of God is like a mustard seed... the kingdom of God is like yeast that a woman took and mixed in with three measures of wheat flour until all was leavened (Lk13:19-21).

The kingdom of heaven on the earth is the living community taking on the mind of essence for accessing the wisdom of intent through the intuition of wholeness... a community ableness made possible through a forgiving community heart... an open community heart with the ever presence of all-inclusive love in the process as we take up our work.

"Hearing" the voice of wisdom – wisdom of intent – and "seeing" intended ways of working – ways of working of life – the whole of life and the wholes within life – the essence community mind is able to lead and guide reason – the reasoning mind of existence – leading to a world of our making congruent with the world of intent. The voice of wisdom enters quietly, enters the quiet; potential lies hidden within, waiting to be seen. They are like the leaven which enables the wheat to become nourishing to life; they are like the mustard seed growing into a dwelling place for the birds... the seed and the leaven essential to becoming, becoming that which is essential to the eternalizing of life on this earth.

We – humanity – have the potential to dwell in the kingdom of heaven... on this earth. We are so intended... essential to fulfilling *the Father's command: Eternal life... on earth as in heaven* (Jn12:50; Mt6:10).

A woman took and mixed... there is a particular role, that being an initiating process role, a role of putting the process in place, a role of leading the creation of a process, a process within community that enables developing the mind of essence, the intuitive mind of essence being the instrument through which the wisdom of intent of the Source and the intended way of working of life are able to enter. The initiating role does not "make" the yeast – that which transmits/carries life to the bread; it sees to it that the "yeast" is added to the wheat flour; the role participates, joins in, becomes an active presence essential to putting the process in place.

Following the Way of Intent: 5

You know how to discern the face of the earth and the sky; how is it you do not discern this time? Why do you not judge for yourselves what is right? (Lk12: 54-57)

Now is the time of potential, the time of intent, the time for co-operating with the intent of the Source and intended ways of working of life.

Now is the time for developing the mind of essence, the mind open to, receptive to the wisdom of intent, the wisdom gift of the Spirit that comes to us through prayerful questioning... petitioning for the seeing of the whole, the intended way of working of the whole, and the seeing of potential, the pattern of intent, the virtue imbedded within at the time life entered. This is the work of the present time... a work made visible through the intuition of wholeness... the intuition of wholeness being the instrument used by the Spirit for wisdom to enter community... wisdom essential to humanity moving towards wholeness, a moving essential to our taking up our intended work of *eternalizing life on the earth* (Jn12:50; Mt6:10)...

Now is the time of great hazard... the hazard of our – humanity's – loss of the capacity for intuition... the hazard to all of life, not merely human life... the hazard to the Source; no life on earth: no souls returning... no life on earth: no spirit manifesting. Soul returning reciprocally nourishes – feeds – the Source; spirit manifesting sustains the intended eternalizing of life on this earth. The hazard being not unlike the time of Mary... only one woman on earth receptive to the Spirit entering... the hazard of now being the soon lost capacity of humanity for intuition, particularly the intuition of wholeness that opens our minds and hearts to Spirit entering, to seeing intent of the Source, to seeing intended ways of working of life... the hazard of the mind of existence completely overtaking and occluding from our accessing, the intuitive mind of essence.

Do we know how to interpret the present times? Will the work of Christ be lost to the original sin, the taking of self as source and the choosing to be led by the tool of existence – reason – over the instrument of essence – intuitive wholeness... leading to our inability to become intentional people of earth, inability for ongoingly fulfilling original intent... *eternal life on earth as in heaven* (Jn12:50; Mt6:10). Do we know how to interpret the present times? The Spirit speaks; will we be open, be prepared to hear, to see? *Why do you not judge for yourselves what is right?*

Martha, burdened with much serving, came to him and said, Lord, do you not care that my sister has left me by myself to do the serving? Tell her to help me. The Lord said to her in reply, Martha, Martha, you are anxious and troubled about many things. There is need of only one thing. Mary has chosen the good part which will not be taken from her (Lk10:38-42).

Have faith that through an open receptive community heart, the Spirit will speak… the Spirit will provide. As living members of life on earth, we have access to, we can live in two worlds – the world of intent and the world of our making. Living in the world of intent calls for the way of Mary… sitting at the feet of Wisdom, taking in – "seeing" and "hearing" – that which is intended, that which is essential – critically essential – to living in congruence with intent of the Source and intended ways of working of life.

Busyness, anxiety and worry about feeding and serving existence, in the absence of being guided by the wisdom of intent and intended ways of working of life, is all for naught. *My food is to do the will of the one who sent me and to accomplish his work* (Jn4:34).

When intent and intended ways of working are guiding our doing, our making, our working, we are truly fed, we are participating fully and truly in eternalizing life.

Mary has chosen the good part. Mary understands that first she must hear and see; then act. Acting without the essential, we are serving existence; serving existence, blind to intent and intended ways becomes a pattern of my will, not Thy will, a pattern of the laws of existence trumping the intent of the Source. Serving essence – the essence pattern of intent of the Source – all are fed. *And it will not be taken from her...* gifts of the Spirit, wisdom gifts will not be taken from her. *All of existence may pass away, but wisdom will never pass away* (Mk13:31).

Serving existence is akin to bees feeding on sugar water. Pollination ends; life – the whole of life – dies... our busy-ness, our worry, our anxiety is our drinking of sugar water: existence being served in the absence of intentionality. Through little reflection, we see the consequences of this now – at this time. Life on earth dying while the hungry mouth of existence is being served. We are anxious, we are worried, we are busy working; but we have no true "answers." They lie in essence... awaiting us to sit together in reflective dialogue at the feet of the Source, engaging in prayerful questioning, opening our community heart and community mind to hearing and seeing... hearing intent of the Source – of the Life – and seeing intended ways of working of life.

Ask and it will be given to you; seek and you will find; knock and it will be opened to you. For everyone asking, receives; and the one seeking, finds; and to the one who knocks, it will be opened (Lk11:9-10).

These words are familiar to many... they seem to come to mind when we are troubled, wish for something, want something. We habitually take these words as asking for something in existence, seeking something we can see, and having access where we are presently closed out; all the time forgetting to read the words only a few lines after... perhaps said only a few moments later, *How much more will the Father in heaven give the holy Spirit to those asking him?* (Lk11:13)

This is a teaching... a teaching about the way of working of the holy Spirit, a teaching of what is called for from us for the accessing of the holy Spirit – the wisdom of the Spirit. This is not a passive process; this is a process of prayerful questioning.

Wisdom enters not unless we ask... unless we are asking seriously. Wisdom comes when we have serious intent. Remembering wisdom is always about intent – intent of the Father and intended way of working of life... wisdom shines light on the whole. To begin, serious intent is not all about us; serious intent is about all – the whole. Seek and you will find. When we seek not, we find not. We can stumble on a few nuggets of learning during our lives; but without engaging in reflection, reflective dialoguing and prayerful questioning, we are not truly seeking and we fail to find; we take what existence-based culture gives us, blind and deaf to the gifts of the Spirit.

Knock and it will be opened. Seeing the whole, seeing the intent – the essence virtue intended by the Source to be unfolded in and through life processes of earth... seeing the intended way of working of life and life processes; that is a door being opened... opened to our intended purpose, work and roles on this earth, opened to *Thy kingdom coming, Thy will being done on earth as in heaven* (Mt6:10).

This is true receiving; this is true finding; this is true opening. All of which call for our serious intent; all of which call for the holy Spirit entering community... bringing to light Jesus' prophesy: *You shall do greater things than these* (Jn14:12).

When they bring you in before the synagogues, the rulers and the authorities, do not be anxious about how or what you shall reply, or what you should answer; for the holy Spirit will teach you in that moment what you must say (Lk12:11-12).

...a profound image of what having faith looks like. For some this appears almost preposterous. Coming from the mind of existence, this which we are being told to do when we are called to defend ourselves seems an insurmountable path to take. And so perhaps we take the option of having a plan; and when everything "works out" according to *our* plan, we thank God and credit the Spirit.

Yet, once we see there is another mind besides the mind of existence, that being the mind of essence, what Christ is telling us to do begins to clarify. We are called to bring with us the mind of essence, the mind of process, the mind that works from intuitive wholeness... the mind prepared, open and receptive to the wisdom of intent of the Source and intended ways of working of life. This is the mind open to, receptive to the teaching of the holy Spirit. The Spirit teaches us what to say... does not tell us what to say... the holy Spirit being teacher of wisdom. With the gift of the Spirit – the gift of the wisdom of intent – reason is then guided/taught... prepared, therefore, to speak. The mind of existence worries about defense; has a plan, sometimes what we call an iron clad plan... leaving no room for the Spirit to enter. The noise of the plan and the worry of the outcome fill the mind of existence; we never hear; we follow my way, not the way of the wisdom of the Spirit.

The ones blaspheming against the holy Spirit will not be forgiven (Mk3:28-29). This one is one who knowingly refuses the path of intent, even curses the path of intent... never hears the wisdom of the Spirit... hence closes self – and often others – from participating in *the Father's command: Life everlasting – on earth as in heaven (Jn12:50; Mt6:10)*.

Turning our backs on the teaching of the Spirit, we fail to see our work and our role – the work and role of humankind – the taking up of which being essential to *Thy will be done on earth as in heaven* (Mt6:10). And we hazard interfering with intent and intended ways... standing in the way of the Spirit; we will never be forgiven. Standing in the way of the Spirit, we are standing in the way of Life, in the way of our – humankind's – work and role in eternalizing life on earth – the taking up of which being the means of building soul for eternal life in heaven, and manifesting spirit eternally available to all of life on earth.

Living life by – leading thinking with and speaking from – the teachings of the Spirit is the intended way of human working... the way of humanity fulfilling our part in eternalizing life on earth.

I came down from heaven not to do my own will but the will of the one who sent me (Jn6:37).

We were brought into this world not to do our own will but the will of the one who created us. *Not my will but Thy will* (Lk22:42).

From the beginning, and ongoingly forever, this is the intended way of working of life. This is the process brought to the world, made visible through seeing the pattern of the process of Christ... and he shares with us the purpose – *eternal life* (Jn12:50). Seeing the pattern of the process of the Son and believing this is the intended pattern, the pattern we are to follow, we enter the work of *Thy kingdom coming, Thy will being done on earth as in heaven* (Mk6:10)... a work which is fueled by and made possible by the love of inclusivity poured onto earth by Christ... a work now, at this time, given direction by the mother's command – *Work for all my children in the world* – a command which awakens and focuses the heart, places the choice of now before us, a choice which, when responded to with a "Yes" of the heart, calls *for two or more gathering in his name* (Mt18:20), building the community mind of essence with the capacity to take up the work... the community mind open to "seeing" – seeing intent of the Source and intended ways of working of the processes of life – the seeing which is purely gift (not of our making), gift of the Spirit. The mind open to and developed by, formed by the love of inclusivity and fed by the Spirit, shows us the way – the path of eternalizing life on this earth, the intended path, the path through which we see our work in the world, build soul, manifest spirit and experience life, experience surrendering to our instrumentality in the intended ongoing unfolding creation. By so doing, we become fully, truly and wholly human, as intended... our souls prepared for returning to the Source on "the last day" and our spirits – the spirit of the manifested virtue – remaining on earth (after our physical death), becoming available to all of life on earth forever.

This develops for us an image of the intended working of *Follow me* (Mt8:22)... *I am...the life* (Jn14:6), an image of the process of following the Life.

We too are commanded *not to lose anything of what the Father has given us* (Jn18:9)... and the Father has given us life. We are expected to take up our work and role in his intended ongoing unfolding of life on this earth. The time is now. *I will raise him on the last day* (Jn6:54) – raise his manifested spirit... to feed life, the ongoingness of life on earth. Raise his soul... to return to and feed the Source; this being the way in which we become reciprocally nourishing within life, the whole of life... reciprocally nourishing with the Life.

My kingdom does not belong to this world… For this I was born and for this I came into the world, to testify to the truth. Everyone who belongs to the truth listens to my voice (Jn18:36-37).

Belonging to this world is belonging to existence… seeing and hearing only that which enters the senses, only that which is verifiable by another's senses. Taking that which enters through existence – *this world* – as the only thing that is real. But there is truly another world… a world not of facts, but a world of truth… a world in which we may live while dwelling on this earth. This too is real… more real and more lasting than the world of existence. We have a choice: To which world will we belong, the world of existence or the world of truth – the world of essence?

Now belonging to truth, to the world of truth, we do not "go out of existence" so to speak; we see and approach existence from a new light – the light of Life. We see that without Life entering, existence runs down. Life entering is the only means of the run-up of existence on the earth. Life is truth. Jesus: *I am the way and the truth and the life (Jn14:6)… Without me, you can do nothing* (Jn15:5). Without me – without *the way and the truth and the life* – you can do nothing.

And so we are called to have faith in Life – not the thing that is alive; but faith in Life, Life which enters existence, faith in the way and the truth of Life. *Everyone who belongs to the truth* – truth of the way, truth of Life – *listens to my voice. The Spirit is my voice.* The Source of truth is not in existence; the Source of life is not in existence. Belonging to the world of truth, the world of Life, we hear his voice… the voice of the Spirit who will *teach us everything and remind us of all told us* (Jn14:26).

Hearing the voice of the Spirit, we receive the gift of truth; the truth of the intent of the Source and the truth of the way... the intended ways of working of life and life's processes on the earth... enabling us to go forth as intentional people of earth, a people who hear the voice and act on the voice; a people who live from truth... a people who take up work and roles in keeping with intent, manifesting intent in the world of existence while living in the world of truth... coming from intent, our daily living becomes *Thy will being done on this earth* (Mt6:10), hence living in the world, fulfilling our intended work in the world but never *belonging* to this world. Belonging to the world of truth, the world of essence; we are taking on the mind of Christ, the process mind of Christ; living in full co-operation with the Source. We the people of earth taking up our role and work in sustaining life and in reciprocally nourishing the whole of life on this earth... as intended. We hear... and the voice teaches us everything, teaches us the way of...

> *Loving God* (Mk12:30), the Source, the Life... the one Source of all life.

> *Loving one another as Christ loved us* (Jn13:34).

> *Eternalizing life... on earth as in heaven* (Jn12:50).

Jesus rejoiced in the holy Spirit and said, Blessed are the eyes that see what you see… Many desired to see what you see, but did not see it, and to hear what you hear, but did not hear it (Lk10:21, 24).

Many desired… What is the difference – the significant distinction – between desiring and surrendering? Between desiring to be the wise on the earth and surrendering to the wisdom of the Source of all? Echoes of Jesus' words to Nicodemus enter… *If you do not believe the Spirit speaks to you, how will you ever believe what is spoken? How will you ever believe what the Spirit speaks to another?* (Jn3:11-12)

Desiring to have access to the secrets of the Source is very different from an act of will, the one ongoing act of will called for in our lives… the surrendering to the intent of the Source… surrendering to our instrumentality, becoming seriously intentional. At this time, the nature of the surrendering is that of community surrendering… community surrendering to instrumentality… community becoming a forgiving heart, an open community heart forgiving other communities – *for they (and we) know not what we do* (Lk23:34)… a forgiveness that opens our heart and turns our mind – opens our community heart to pursuing that which works for all children in the world and turns our community mind to the wisdom of wholeness, intentionally moving towards wholeness, away from that which divides, moving towards wholeness of humanity and the wholeness of all life on this earth… of which humanity is an intended living member.

This is the essential shift – the change in heart and mind – that opens our community heart to all-inclusive love of Christ and opens our community mind to seeing and to hearing – to seeing and hearing gifts of the Spirit – hearing the intent of the Source for life on earth and seeing intended ways of working of life.

And so we see more clearly now: The entry of such gifts are revealed to the *childlike* (Lk10:21)... the *wise and learned* being the "expert" in the mind of existence, while the *childlike* realize that no matter how wise, no matter how learned, if our path is not formed and fueled by all-inclusive love, and led by the wisdom gifts of intent and intended ways of working... if the path we take is not the path of instrumentality; we are truly blind; we are truly deaf... unable to take up our work and role within the whole of life on this earth at this time as intended... as community, as nation, as a people of earth.

Following the Way of Intent: 12

Jesus said to his disciples, Not everyone who says to me, Lord, Lord, will enter the kingdom of heaven, but only the one who does the will of my Father in heaven (Mt 7:21).

A very brief and powerful description of the essence of the way of entering the kingdom of heaven. Jesus uses here, the word, "only"... taking things to essence... *only the one who does the will of my Father in heaven... will enter into the kingdom of heaven.*

We are reminded, as we read these words, of the prophesy embedded in the Lord's Prayer to the Father, *Thy kingdom come, Thy will be done on earth as in heaven* (Mt6:10). How do we enter into the kingdom? By doing the will of the Father in heaven... this is living in the kingdom *on earth as in heaven.*

We are taken to the words of Christ, words to his disciples just before his death, that he would ask the Father to send to them the holy Spirit (Jn14:15-18)... the holy Spirit being essential to the ongoing seeing and understanding of the will – the intent – of the Father... ongoing as the life processes on earth unfold... a seeing and understanding essential to our *building a house on rock* (Mt7:24). Rock is wisdom – the wisdom gift of the Spirit. Building our lives on wisdom – the will of the Father in heaven ongoingly available to us through the Spirit – we enter and live in *the kingdom, on this earth as in heaven.*

Amazingly, in this world in which we believe to be the strongest, that which is "solid as rock"; we hear that dwelling in the kingdom on earth, we are only rock when we see and understand the will of the Father – through wisdom gifts of the Spirit – and build from wisdom... doing the will of the Father; we are only strong when we are prayerfully receptive.

All of which is bringing us back to the essentiality of having an open forgiving community heart, and the will to take up the work of developing the community mind of essence, a mind that sources all, builds all, from the intent of the Source – the Father of all life, the Father of all.

Jesus tells us, he is not fooled by mighty deeds in his name. There is only one thing that leads to the kingdom – that is doing the will of the Father. Building life on this rock, the rock of the wisdom of intent of the Source and intended ways of working of life, is the means of entering the kingdom. Building life on this rock, we must listen to the voice of the Spirit and build from there. The Spirit will tell us all that we need... when we *have the ears to hear and the eyes to see* (Lk10:23-24). The wisdom council of the Spirit will guide us in all managing of existence; when existence leads our thinking, wisdom is silenced and we are building our house on sand.

Two blind men. Then he touched their eyes and said, Let it be done for you according to your faith. And their eyes were opened (Mt9:29).

A seemingly simple little story, yet one that holds significant teaching. Wholeness enters through faith... faith that we will be given all that we need – we will "see" all that we need – to go forth, to carry out the work of our heart, our intended work on this earth, our work which sustains life and is reciprocally nourishing within the whole of life.

Significant is two blind men, leading our memory to *Where two or more are gathering in my name, so there shall I be* (Mt18:20). Faith in the essence of Christ – all-inclusive love – is what is being asked about in this going forward gospel; what is being asked for. Community – two or more – having faith... faith which manifests in opening the heart, opening which enables, is essential to, all-inclusive love entering... the particular nature of love – love from above, not man's love – essential to our "seeing" – seeing and understanding that which is essential for taking up our work and living our role as human community within the whole of life on this earth... and by so doing, we are joining in the reciprocally nourishing processes of life, taking our part in *eternalizing life on earth as in heaven* (Jn12:50).

Two or more...

Gathering in the name of all-inclusive love...

Two or more with faith, with a fully open heart, receptive heart, forgiving heart – open forgiving community heart.

Love entering – all-inclusive love entering…

Enabling our taking up work in ways that work for all children in the world…

Enabling our taking our part in eternalizing life on earth as in heaven.

Through and by our work within the whole of life, work of two of more gathering in the name of all-inclusive love, we manifest community spirit, spirit ongoingly available to all of life on earth… becoming reciprocally nourishing within the whole of life.

Images of the working of the mustard seed return. *The kingdom of heaven on earth is like a mustard seed* (Lk13:19)… faith the size of a mustard seed ongoingly nourishing the ongoingness, everlastingness of life on earth… as in heaven.

To what shall I compare this generation? It is like children who sit in marketplaces and call to one another, "We played the flute for you, but you did not dance, we sang a dirge but you did not mourn…" Wisdom is vindicated by her works (Mt 11:16-19).

Christ speaks of a generation of no heart… no tendencies to experience and embrace joy (*We played the flute but you did not dance*), no tendencies/capacity to experience sorrow (*We sang the dirge but you did not mourn*). Like children who see we are not experiencing the agonies and ecstasies of life… yet with no compassion for one another.

Christ, experiencing such, was touched by those who were truly struggling with life, fully aware of the agonies and ecstasies, the sorrows and the joys… those whose wish it was to become whole. He was not as a schoolyard child, sitting on the curb, scorning others for having no feelings while they themselves did not see or understand. No, Christ shows us the way. Organize yourself with all-inclusive love and follow the path that wisdom provides. Begin with wisdom, not with scorn or attack; not from ignorance. Wisdom is to lead our works. When wisdom leads, our works which follow are on the path of intent, the intent of the Father, the Source of all…

Are we a generation that criticizes what we see in existence while failing to develop the mind of essence, failing to open our hearts to wisdom, failing to answer "Yes" to wisdom leading our thinking, to wisdom leading our works?

Wisdom may not be understood by this generation, but *she is vindicated by her works*.

If you do not believe what I say, at least believe my works (Jn10:37-38).

In the beginning was the word... all things came to be through him, and without him nothing came to be. What came to be through him was life (Jn1:1, 3-4).

Reflecting on these words from the mind of essence, we begin to "see," to gain an image of, the process expressed. Remembering process is hidden; structure is visible. Process is that which unfolds essence, that which is essential to manifesting essence on this earth... process being essential to our manifesting spirit as we live our lives on this earth.

What came to be through the word was life. Without life, nothing comes into being. *Coming into being* gives us an image of an upwardly advancing unfolding. Through life there is a coming into being, an upwardly advancing unfolding. Without life, there is a running down.

In today's world, we – humankind – manipulate the conditions favorable to life entering. Some even think of ourselves as the source, when manipulating life processes for self-serving needs, or even for some segmented "good," without really contemplating life itself – the intent of life, life which is from the Life.

Life is that which enters existence and enables run-up... enables the organizing of existence into higher order more complex organisms, organisms and systems of organizing with the capacity to grow and to develop, to cure and to mend. As we observe our own bodies, we see cuts heal, colds mend, infants develop into adults, etc. We can be on the verge of death, but if life persists, we again become whole, we are healed by life... the will force, the powers of life.

Somehow, mistakenly, we have come to view it our task, our right, to subdue earth. Reflection tells us earth was created for life to have a place to enter into the working of the universe. If there is any subduing to be done, it would be to take up work that subdues that which interferes with the intended everlastingness of life on this earth... the everlasting of the whole of life, not solely human life.

What came to be through the word was life. Without the intent of the Source, without the ongoing will of the Source, life does not enter. The earth would not be a living planet; without life, earth would be a dead planet. Life enters to overcome death; to overcome rundown. Life continues the run-up process of the intended eternal unfolding creation. Without Life, nothing comes to be; particularly that is, life on earth ends – that which we see with the senses and call life ends without Life entering.

Hence, the essentiality of our taking up the work, the reflective work, of reading the gospels from the perspective of *I am the Life* (Jn14:6), from the perspective of the life of the whole, the whole of life... reflective work which holds the promise of revealing going forward guidance for living on this earth as full and true members of life, members who understand we too (along with all of life) have work and roles in making real *everlasting life on earth as in heaven* (Jn12:50; Mt6:10). Our having choice is not only the source of the uniqueness of ourselves relative to other members of life, but adds complexity to our work. For our choice is either to subdue and extract from life – serving self, serving that to which self is attached, that with which self is identified – or to reciprocally nourish life, the whole of life, the life of the whole – serving the Source. Choosing to serve the Source is manifested in embracing our instrumentality... letting go of "our plans" and "God has a plan" and joining in and with intent, with the everlasting life on earth intent of the Source, of the Life. A path of choice for which Christ provides a pattern… the pattern of the process… the process of being about the affairs of the Father… the Father's affairs being that of ongoing run-up, advancing of the whole of life on earth… *eternal life on earth as in heaven.* To this we are, each and all, called to answer "Yes."

Following the Way of Intent: 16

Teacher, where are you staying? Come… Follow me… and you will see (Jn1:38-39).

Come… follow me… and you will see – see with your mind and heart, not with your eyes. Follow *the way, the truth and the life* (Jn14:6); follow the path, the pattern of my life; take up the work of life from the truth of my way and you will see where I am staying.

Blessed are those with eyes that can see and ears that can hear (Mt13:16).

Where are you staying? Jesus stayed in the mind of essence; he did not stay in the mind of existence. He stayed in the world of intent… of the Source; and intended ways of working of life… and with his every act coming from all-inclusive love, he brought intent and intended ways of life into the world of existence… showing us both where we are to be staying and the path essential to follow to enable our staying.

A few words from Proverbs (9:1-6) add to our image of coming from the mind of essence. *Wisdom calls from the heights out over the city: Let whoever is simple turn in here; to him who lacks understanding, I say, Come, eat of my food, and drink of the wine I have mixed! Forsake foolishness that you may live; advance in the way of understanding.*

True understanding, of course, being wisdom, the wisdom of intent and intended ways of working of life.

Repent, for the kingdom of heaven is at hand (Mt4:17).

A few words; yet containing the declaration of the potential, the intended advancement in humankind; the potential – *the kingdom of heaven – is at hand,* at the door; the age
of the kingdom on earth as in heaven becoming open and
available to all.

And the first change, the change we must make, is to repent
(metanoia in Greek)... to change heart and mind, to
change the perspective from which we view the world, turn
hearts to that which works for all children in the world and
turn minds to the wisdom of Thy will – the wisdom of
intent and intended ways of life. This is the first step. Let
go of self as source, self as in control, self as having the
answers; enter the process reflected in the first beatitude:
*Blessed are communities poor in spirit, because of them is the
kingdom of heaven* (Mt5:3). Metanoia was the first "move"
then; metanoia is the first move now. With this metanoia,
with this change in heart and mind, the kingdom of heav-
en is at hand. This turning of heart and mind creates,
brings into being, the receptivity essential for eyes that can
see and ears that can hear (Lk10:23-24)... "eyes" of the
mind and "ears" of the heart. This change calls for faith;
faith in what we hear and what we see... faith in what is
given to our hearts and minds when we let go of self as
source and let go of reason over wisdom.

When we enter this world of seeing and hearing, the kingdom of heaven is at hand... *Thy kingdom come, Thy will be
done on earth as in heaven* (Mt6:10).

Following the Way of Intent: 18

He went off to the mountain to pray (Lk6:12).

He separated himself from the world of our making – to pray… to enter the mind of essence… the mind open and receptive to accessing the intent of the Source and intended ways of working of life. Prayer… the opening of the receptive "space" – the opening of the heart and mind to intent… the fruits of which are seeing, and sometimes hearing… being given by the Spirit of truth the wisdom we need – wisdom of intent – for going forward on this earth, for living our lives in ways congruent with the intent of the Source, living our lives in ways reciprocally nourishing within the whole of life, ways in keeping with the intent of the Father; *the Father's command being life everlasting* (Jn12:50). *And he went off to the mountain to pray*… the prayer being (as we were given) *Thy kingdom come, Thy will be done, as in heaven, also on this earth* (Mt6:9-13)… a prayer asking the Father for the wisdom gift of intent and intended ways of working of life…. asking the Father for all-inclusive love, the love essential to forgiveness.

My food is to do the will of the Father and take up his work (Jn4:34).

Give us this day our essential bread… our bread, the bread of Life, being the *doing of the will of the Father, the taking up of his work*… doing possible by and through the gift of wisdom, wisdom accessible through the Spirit of wisdom, wisdom available to open hearts… open forgiving community hearts with serious intent to take up/cooperate with the work of the Father. *My food is to do the will of the Father and take up his work*… possible for humanity, possible for community, if we lead with *going off to the mountain to pray*.

133

Whoever blasphemes against the holy Spirit will never have for-giveness, but is guilty of an everlasting sin (Mk3:28-29).

Essence virtue is the means of seeing what is at the heart of something... that which is enfolded, intended to be unfold-ed. The essence virtue of Christ is love – all-inclusive love... loving inclusively being the process of our partici-pating with the intended unfolding of the essence virtue of Christ on this earth. The essence virtue of the Life is life... eternally upwardly unfolding life. We are becoming one with the Life, the Father of life, as we authentically embrace and take up our work and role in eternalizing upwardly unfolding life... fulfilling *the Father's command – everlasting life – on this earth as in heaven* (Jn12:50; Mt6:10). And the essence virtue of the Spirit is wisdom – wisdom essential to intentionally working. Whoever blasphemes against the Spirit blasphemes against intentionally working... against all working congruent with the intended eternal upward unfolding of life itself, of the life of the whole, of the whole of life on this earth. The Spirit, the accessing of the wisdom gifts of the Spirit, the seeing of the intended way of work-ing of life, is essential to our ongoingly fulfilling our intend-ed work and role as members of earth's life community. Blaspheming against the Spirit is interfering – knowingly interfering – with intentionally working, with the intended ongoing unfolding of life itself. For *the Father's command-ment is eternal life... as in heaven, so also on the earth.*

No one enters the strong man's house to plunder his property without first tying up the strong man (Mk3:27). Blaspheming the Spirit is tying up the strong man. Silencing the Spirit, closing the heart and mind to the Spirit, we plunder the house... we plunder life, life which comes from the Life, the Source of life.

The Father's command is eternal life... on this earth... here and in the unfolding now. To take up this work calls for our seeing, embracing and cooperating with intended ways of life – intended ways of the working of the processes of life. The seeing comes first... seeing which comes to us through the Spirit. He who blasphemes against the Spirit – tying up one's own and others' capacity to see, tying up the community's ableness to see – ultimately plunders the house. For without guiding the world of our making with the wisdom of intent and intended ways of life, intended ways of working of life, we ultimately plunder the Father's house. Life itself – the purpose for which earth was created – will end. The everlasting sin is taking the living earth as ours to plunder, as ours to extract from, to lord over, to subdue. The Spirit was sent to guide us with truth, the truth essential for our work, the work by and through which it becomes possible for us to fully and truly participate in fulfilling *the Father's commandment, everlasting life. Hence blaspheming against the holy Spirit – tying up the strong man and plundering the Father's house – being an everlasting sin.* A sobering realization.

Following the Way of Intent: 20

This is how it is with the kingdom of God; it is as if a man were to scatter seed on the land... and the seed would sprout and grow, he knows not how. Of its own accord the land yields fruit... And when the grain is ripe, he wields the sickle at once, for the harvest has come (Mk 4:26-29).

The kingdom of heaven – on earth as in heaven – is a kingdom of life. We are expected, actually intended participants, in the process of life, in the intended eternally upwardly unfolding of life... intended to "scatter seeds," to scatter seeds of life. The honeybee is an instrument for pollination within the whole of life. While the honeybee goes about its business, the business of building, feeding, caring for and sustaining the hive, unknowingly, the bee is "scattering seeds," enabling the intended ongoingness of life, the whole of life, through pollination. We too, being members of life, are intended instruments in the process of eternalizing life on earth, instruments in the ongoingness of the kingdom on earth. While we go about our daily doings, we too are intended to "scatter seeds of life." Obviously for humankind, unlike the honeybee, there is something called conscious choice. We have the choice to scatter seeds or not. Consciously choosing – choosing possible with consciousness, choosing possible through the seeing of intended wholeness, intended ways of life – we are answering "Yes" to *loving one another as I have loved you* (Jn13:34), followed by "Yes" to *Thy will being done on earth as in heaven* (Jn12:50; Mt6:10). The first yes opening our hearts and minds to becoming instruments of love... instruments of the all-inclusive love of Christ – to loving inclusively; and the second yes to becoming instruments of the Spirit, instruments of work, intentionally working in congruence with the intended ways of life, the intended way of working of life's processes. Choosing yes to all-inclusive love is like the seed scattered on the ground; choosing yes to intentionally working, we are co-operating with life, becoming reciprocally nourishing within the whole of life in intended ways, perhaps un-seeable for us, and yet fully essential to the ongoingness of life on this earth, fully essential to *Thy kingdom coming* – ongoingly coming – on *earth as in heaven*... fully essential to our fulfilling the Father's command of life – *eternal life* (Jn12:50) – *on earth as in heaven.*

Humankind must scatter the seed; seed which sprouts and grows, *he knows not how. Of its own accord the land yields fruit.* We are not the source of life... we are instruments, intended instruments in the intended eternal unfolding of life... instruments loving inclusively and intentionally working... loving inclusively and working from and through intent being the means by which we take up our intended work and roles in the eternalizing of upwardly unfolding life... the only means by which there will be a harvest... harvest not for the self, but to sustain the eternal upwardly unfolding of the whole of life itself... fulfilling the ongoing intent of the Source... one Source, all else instruments.

Following the Way of Intent: 21

Unless a grain of wheat falls to the ground and dies, it remains just a grain of wheat, but if it dies, it produces much fruit. Whoever loves his life loses it, and whoever hates his life in this world will preserve it for eternal life. Whoever serves me must follow me, and where I am, there also will my servant be. The Father will honor whoever serves me (Jn12:24-26).

Dying to self, dying to self-centeredness – *being poor in spirit* (Mt5:3) – begins the process of producing much fruit... fruit which reciprocally nourishes life. Whoever loves his life – is attached to the world of existence; will not enter the mind of essence – loses life... loses eternal life, on earth as in heaven. Whoever hates his life in this world – hates being attached to, determined by, conformed with the world of existence – will preserve it, preserve life eternally.

It is not all about us. It is not all about human life; but the ongoingness of life, the whole of life, of which we – humankind – are members. Habitually, we view the above words of Christ from the mind of existence, the reasoning mind of existence, the mind dependent upon the senses for determining what is real... and habitually with our eye on the hereafter; that is on what is being told in this teaching from the perspective of our gaining salvation.

Here, in this reflection, we are viewing these words of Jesus from a life of the whole perspective and with the mind of essence... enabling us – through the intuition of wholeness and intentional dialogue – to gain an image of that which is being taught – the process being taught – for our living as intentional members of life on this earth in the here and unfolding now... imaging which enables us to put on, to live, the process of Christ... for our becoming in the way of Christ, the way of intent.

138

Continuing this reflection, it is useful for us to hold in mind the truths…

The perspective we hold, where we start our thinking from,
determines the path we take, the direction we move in,
what we move towards, what we move away from.

And the second truth…

If love is not present in the process,
love will not be present in the outcomes…

Along with holding in mind the essential words of Jesus: *I am the way and the truth and the life* (Jn14:6) – *I am the way and the truth of Life; I am… the Life.*

What is the process of life on this earth, the process that sustains the eternal ongoing unfolding life? A process we are enabled to image through the words, *unless a grain of wheat falls to the ground and dies, it remains just a grain of wheat, but if it dies, it produces much fruit.* This image takes us to seeing the working of the feeding of life… one grain of wheat, if it dies, produces much fruit – fruit intended to feed the many; fruit which does feed the many; and as well fruit enough such that more might fall to the ground and again produce much fruit. This one sentence provides an image of the process of life, of the Life, of the way of working of life on and through this earth, of Life's intended way of working of life. Now we notice that Jesus uses the word, *unless* – a significant word, a word which deepens our understanding of a parable told by Christ of a man who hoarded grain (Lk12:16-21). Keeping all the grain for food, to feed self, to serve self, to serve existence without producing fruit to feed the whole of life, to feed all of life on earth, we ourselves remain just a grain of wheat… and the fruit intended in support of the eternalizing of life does not come into

139

being. Yes, our existence mind might know this, we may have studied about its working in biology; but have we seen with clarity, the implications in relation to ourselves – implications beyond our aim to sustain ourselves, beyond the life of humankind? Have we seen what is being said here about our purpose, work and role on this earth… and our choices in that regard?

He takes us further: *Whoever loves his life loses it, and whoever hates his life in this world will preserve it for eternal life.* Whoever loves his life, whoever clings to being a grain of wheat, clings to being externally defined by an existence-based culture, ultimately loses it… is eaten, rots, falls on poor soil, etc. Whoever hates his life in this world, turns his back on clinging to self as a grain, lets go of self as source; whoever becomes *poor in spirit,* whoever lets go of his seedness realizes that within is life, life intended for transformation, the grain intended to become a wheat shaft and bear fruit, becomes an active participant, a conscious instrument in preserving life for the eternalizing of life on earth. Some grain sustains the now of life of humanity; some grain falls to the ground and dies so that much fruit may be produced… so that the intended ongoing upwardly unfolding of life on this earth – eternalizing of life on and through earth – continues.

Letting go of our attachments to the world of existence, moving into the world of essence is a true shift, a commitment, a choice… to take up our Father's work, to take up work and role in preserving life, for eternal life… a shift calling for dying to the self – community becoming poor in spirit – and turning to the work of eternalizing life on earth as in heaven – work that works for all children in the world; work that brings into being a world of our making congruent with the world of intent; work that moves us towards wholeness and oneness, away from that which divides. And

140

the beauty is, by so doing, we build the soul and spirit of humanity; soul and spirit preserved for eternal life on earth and in heaven. True beauty.

Ask and it will be given to you; seek and you will find; knock and the door will be opened to you. For everyone who asks, receives; and the one who seeks finds; and the one who knocks, the door will be opened (Mt7:7-8).

This is a promise... a promise to those with serious intent, those whose wish it is to be and become intentional... those who have chosen the path of intent and are serious about taking that path... those who, with all their heart, with all their mind, with all their strength and soul are intent on being and becoming intentional.

And where does this path begin? With asking, seeking and knocking... with pursuing a seeing... pursuing seeing intent, seeing intended ways of life, intended ways of working of life. The seeing is pure gift, gift of the Spirit, wisdom gift of the Spirit... wisdom gift available to us, ongoingly present; but we must ask, seek, knock... and have faith that that which we need will be given. We will see and hear that which we need for our intentionally working, working in full congruence with the intent of the Life, the intent of the Source of life.

Good things are given by the Father to those who ask him (Mt7:11). Good things being the wisdom of the Spirit and the all-inclusive love of Christ, essential to our taking up the Father's work – the way of *eternalizing life... on earth as in heaven* (Jn12:50; Mt6:10).

In praying, do not babble like the pagans, who think that they will be heard because of their many words. Do not be like them. Your Father knows what you need before you ask him (Mt6:7-8).

The Father is the Life… the Source of life on earth. We, humankind are members of life – intentional members of life. All members of life have needs for the sustaining of life… and have work and roles within and with regard to the whole of life. The Father – the Author of life – who is the Life and *commands eternal life – on earth as in heaven* (Jn12:50; Mt6:10) – knows what we need to sustain the responsibilities of our livingness and to fulfill our work and roles in becoming reciprocally nourishing within the whole of life.

The Father knows that to take up and carry out our work, the particular work of now, work of fulfilling our – humankind's – intentional purpose with regard to the life of the whole, calls for the all-inclusive love of Christ and the wisdom of the Spirit. We must become instruments of all-inclusive love… and see and understand intended ways of life on this earth… enabling our creating an active presence of a work for all children – all children of life, all children of the living world – culture… enabling the world of our making becoming congruent with the world of intent, congruent with the intended ways of working of life on this earth at this time.

The Father knows what we need before we ask him… what we need for *Thy kingdom coming and Thy will being done on this earth…* what we need for taking up our intended work on earth – as originally intended before we turned our backs on the Source, on wisdom and on our membership in life on this earth.

Hence our prayer is not to be the babble of many words, but the clearing away of self, the becoming poor in spirit, and at this time of potential, the opening of the community self to the work and roles before us and asking for what the Father knows we need to take up the work of now.

For the truth is, the sustaining of one's own physical life can be done in congruence with the intended eternal upward unfolding of the whole of life on earth, or by extracting from and subduing life; the sustaining of one's own life can be to the detriment of the children of the world, or we can go the way of congruence with the intent of the Source and intended ways of working of life and of taking up pursuits in ways that work for all children. The choice is ours. Choosing the latter calls for the all-inclusive love of Christ and the gifts of the Spirit, the gifts of seeing the intended ways of life. Yes, *the Father knows what we need before we ask.*

Following the Way of Intent: 24

When the wedding wine ran short, the mother of Jesus said to him, They have no wine. Jesus said to her, Woman, how does your concern affect me? My hour has not yet come. His Mother said to the servers, Do whatever he tells you (Jn2:3-5).

The gospels seem to be full of these short interactions... sometimes more seeming to have the purpose of setting the stage for that which is to come – serving as the introduction – than to impart a teaching. The situation which has presented itself is one of embarrassment to the wedding hosts. Surely it would be embarrassing to invite many people to a wedding and then run out of wine. The mother of Jesus wished to ward off, save or rescue them from such embarrassment, and perhaps as well to keep the celebration alive... apparently wishing that Jesus would use his special gifts to solve the problem. Jesus' response is very interesting. He addresses his mother as *woman*. Not a way, even in today's age of coarseness, to address one's mother. He is responding to her as someone whose thinking is stuck in the world of existence, not seeing or coming from the intent of the Father, the Source of all. He asks, *How does this concern affect me?* Jesus' work, all sourced in intent, would certainly not be concerned with social customs, with upholding cultural ways, with using his gifts for keeping a party going. This is not his work. This is not the purpose of his gifts. Hence we hear the further response, *My hour has not yet come.* The hour, his hour would be the time of taking up and fulfilling the work to which he was called, the work for which he came into this world. One might conclude or surmise that his ultimate affirmative response to her request was not due to holding off embarrassment, but from the love for his mother and compassion for people – for lost souls.

Jesus tells us *Follow me* (Mt8:22). Follow his path... his

path being led by the intent of the Father, the work for which he was sent, work of fulfilling the purpose for which he came to earth. We too have work, intentional work, our called work, the work of our heart, work we come to see and understand through prayerful questioning, the intuition of wholeness and reflective dialoguing, a complete opening of self to the seeing that comes… a seeing that calls for letting go of serving self, and answering "Yes" to the will of the Father. This seeing is on a path of moving towards wholeness… towards seeing ourselves as intended members in the whole of life, with intended work and roles in that regard. Hence, the seeing of our called work, the work of the heart, calls for our taking a life of the whole perspective and accessing the wisdom of intent through intuitive wholeness and the mind of essence. This is the disciplining of the mind called for, along with the opening of the heart. Through the disciplining of mind and opening of heart, we begin to see intent and intended ways of life… and our intended work and roles within life… a seeing of Thy will, not my will. Hence calling for choice, conscious choice on our part… choice to take up the work of our *hour*, our intentional purpose… and let go of being determined and led by cultural patterns that have little meaning as far as the eternal ongoingness of life. As we think about it, we readily see that running out of wine at a wedding is inconsequential to life, life of the whole.

Yet, there is something that is consequential, that which makes it possible to take up our work and roles in ways congruent with the intent of the Source… that something is love – the all-inclusive love of Christ.

With this happening, which falls in the beginning of Jesus' ministry, we see him indexing to, calling attention to his purpose – his reason for living on this earth… and responding from and through all-inclusive love. We too are called to follow *the way* (Jn14:6)... take up and live from our intentional purpose, not our preferred or desired goals, and become instruments of the all-inclusive love of Christ, making possible the forgiving open heart essential to taking up our work.

Reflecting on what is written here, we notice much is about self. The process of becoming poor in spirit – of letting go of self and self-centeredness – is an initiating step on the path of intent, a step that has imbedded within it the realization of our intended membership in community. Yet, at this time of now we are seeing and experiencing something that can be called the community self – communities of people with attachments to ideas and solutions, to ideologies that are incomplete and fragmented, that are exacerbating and feeding divisiveness. The individual self, becoming attached to and identified with these ideologies, joins in the divisiveness, divisiveness which leads to anger, meanness and ultimately, to hate. At this time of now, what is called for is *community* letting go of self, community *becoming poor in spirit*, community heart becoming forgiving and open... community becoming instrument for all-inclusive love entering and manifesting on this earth. One way we might say this is that "being a good person" is no longer enough; as community we must become instrument of all-inclusive love taking up the work of *Thy will being done on this earth* (Mt6:10)... work which at this time takes and sustains its direction with the mother's command – *Work for all my children in the world* – and grounds itself in the work of *bringing the world of our making into congruence with the world of intent.*

Reflecting on this teaching of Christ, we see and experience an interchange between existence and essence, between the world of our making and the world of intent, between leading from cultural status and leading from intentional purpose; we see and realize we are being introduced to the work now before us; the community work now before us.

The kingdom of God will be taken from you and given to a nation producing its fruit (Mt21:43).

We are, each and all, intended to become reciprocally nourishing within the whole of life, as intended working members of the life of the whole. We are to bear fruit that reciprocally nourishes the whole... the whole of life on this earth. To become reciprocally nourishing, we must become – as nations – fruit bearers, fruit producers... producers of fruit which feeds life of all nations, fruit which feeds and nourishes all of life, of which humanity is a member. Each nation on this earth has access to, receives the gift of particular natures of earth's resources, resources which are a part of earth itself, as well as to natures of life processes particular to our place on earth, life processes which are essential to the ongoingness of the whole of life (seasons, rain systems, ocean currents and migration patterns, come to mind).

And so, the work which presents itself to us is twofold. The work of sustaining and improving our existence (think of the honeybee building and maintaining the hive, gathering nectar to feed the hive), and the work of nourishing, enabling the life of the whole, the whole of life (pollination). "Reciprocally nourishing" brings to us the image of being nourishing within the whole of life in ways that reciprocally enable our sustaining the ongoingness of our own lives, the lives of our families, communities, nations. We need not subdue earth and extract from the whole of life for "feeding our families" (making honey with sugar water, bypassing pollination, for example). We need *bear fruit that lasts* (Jn15:16). What is intended by the Father, the Source, the Life, the Source of life, is that we work in intentional ways with love – all-inclusive love – in our hearts. This work, this way of working – intentionally working – bears fruit that lasts, fruit which ongoingly feeds *the eternalizing of life on this earth* (Jn12:50; Mt6:10)... as intended.

Diminishing life, extracting from life, interfering with the intended ways of life, intended ways of working of life, is truly nonsensical, and counterintuitive. We are "killing life so that we may live." The guiding words, *I desire mercy, not sacrifice* (Mt12:7), come to mind. Have mercy for all life. Not sacrifice. Do not sacrifice life of the whole in order to build up a divisive, segmented life for self.

Looking at the world from the frame of reference of our nation's current culture – a culture based on, built from, a particular world view, a fragmented world view – we argue this is not possible. We need things to be able to live. Leading to our asking if this is where we want to stay, wish to stay? Is this where we are intended to stay? A true shift, the beginnings of preparing ourselves for a true and real shift, lies in our seeing and realizing we have a very fragmented and fragmenting world view. Reflecting on our current world view leads us to finding ourselves attached to ideologies, not being led by a living philosophy, a philosophy in keeping with intent and intended ways... finding ourselves attached to a world of our making and a way of making our world moving us away from congruence with the eternalizing of life and away from that which works for all children in the world.

"Seeing ourselves clearly" is the place – the narrow gate – of entering the new space, entering the space of *Thy will being done on this earth* (Mt6:10), the kingdom space of *bearing fruit that lasts...* work essentially fueled and enabled by and through all-inclusive love in our processes, work possible by and through the wisdom gifts of the Spirit – the gift of seeing intent and intended ways of life; work that calls for our answering "Yes"… and never looking back.

It seems we are beginning to gain a working image of what it means to be *community poor in spirit who make up the kingdom of heaven* (Mt5:3) and what it means for a nation – of which we are a living part – *to bear fruit that lasts*, taking up ongoing community work in the intended eternal upwardly unfolding life on this earth… bearing fruit fulfilling *the Father's command: eternal life* (Jn12:50).

Blessed are the communities poor in spirit, because of them is the kingdom of heaven.

Blessed are the communities who are mourning, for they shall be comforted.

Blessed are the meek communities, because they shall inherit the earth.

Blessed are the communities who are hungering and thirsting after righteousness, because they shall be satisfied.

Blessed are the merciful communities, because they shall receive mercy.

Blessed are the communities pure in heart, because they shall see God.

Blessed are the peacemaking communities, because they shall be called children of God.

Blessed are the communities being persecuted because of righteousness, for of them is the kingdom of heaven.

Blessed are you, communities, when they shall reproach you, and persecute you, and shall say every evil word against you, lying, on account of me. Rejoice and be very glad, for the reward of you shall be great in heaven; for they thus persecuted the prophets before you (Mt5:3-12).

This time of now, this time of advancing our humanness, this time of taking up the way of intent, calls for our shifting perspective...

Shifting from a human centered to the life of the whole centered perspective; life of the whole including humanity, yet reaching to the whole of life within which humanity is a living member. The life of the whole perspective brings humanity closer to seeing as the Father – the Source of life – sees.

Shifting from seeing self as the smallest whole to seeing

community as the smallest whole. The work of now, the work essential to advancing our humanness, work calling for our intentionally following the *Father's eternal life commandment* (Jn12:50), becomes possible, is possible with and through our seeing community is the smallest whole; the processing within community – intentional dialoguing, prayerful questioning – being the means of opening hearts and minds to accessing and seeing intent and intended ways of the unfolding life processes… preparing community members for going out into the world guided by this seeing and understanding, taking up roles in the work of bringing the world of our making into congruence with the world of intent.

At this time of now, this perspective shift is essential to our seeing the way of intent.

Within Christ's teachings, he left for us a process we have come to call the beatitudes. The beatitudes, when viewed as an unfolding community process, provide a seeing of, as well as a means of deepening understanding of the way of intent. Seeing the beatitudes as process calls for our letting go of our self-focused human centered perspective… calls for community reflecting together in intentional dialogue from the life of the whole perspective, building an image of the intended unfolding beingness and willfulness of community as we live and work from the beatitudes. (For purposes of intentional community dialogue, it may be useful to draw a circle, place one dot on the top of the circle plus eight dots evenly spaced around the circle. At about the "one o'clock" position, write the first beatitude… following around clockwise, write in the remaining beatitudes.)

Blessed are the communities poor in spirit, because of them is the kingdom of heaven. Being poor in spirit is the essential place to begin… taking us all the way back to our original failings

153

in the garden where we took ourselves as source and embraced reason, our capacity for reasoning, over wisdom. Since then, the struggles of humanity have all harkened back to taking self as source and reason dominating wisdom. Blessed are the *communities* poor in spirit. Blessed are those communities embracing the truth, *one Source and all else instruments*. Embracing such truth leads to seeing that life is intended to be led by the way of wisdom, the wisdom of intent. The reasoning mind of existence, being fragmented and fragmenting, has insufficient capacity to lead in ways participating fully and intentionally in eternalizing life.

At this time, the time of advancing our humanness by and through the shift to seeing community as the smallest whole and coming from the life of the whole perspective while taking on the intuitive mind of essence, all the beatitudes speak to community: Blessed are the communities poor in spirit; blessed are the communities who are mourning; blessed are the meek communities, and so on. Blessed are the communities poor in spirit, the communities that do not take themselves as source, the communities that see themselves as instrument. Blessed are the communities that, through intentional dialogue and prayerful questioning, open their hearts and minds to seeing process and seeking wholeness… seeing and seeking that creates a space for Spirit entering with gifts of wisdom – wisdom of intent and intended ways – wisdom for leading and guiding the work and way of working of the community. Blessed are such communities. These have access to seeing the intended way of the kingdom; these make visibly present the process of *Thy kingdom coming on the earth* (Mk6:10).

Blessed are communities who are mourning, for they shall be comforted. Jesus' words, *I am the way and the truth and the life* (Jn14:6), come to mind. Blessed are the communities mourning the loss of life, the loss of the one life, the loss of the eternal ongoing upwardly unfolding whole of life. Blessed are the communities seeing life... seeing the whole of life and the life of the whole... seeing living humanity as an intentional living member of the whole of life on earth... seeing children, all children in the world as being intentional members of the whole of life, members with intended purpose, work and roles within the whole of life. Blessed are the communities that mourn the degradation, the diminishing, the loss of life. Blessed are communities that see, understand, and take to heart the wonder, the beauty, the awe of life and as well, see, understand and take to heart the loss of life ... the loss for each, the loss for all, the loss for the whole. The communities with hearts open to all children, the communities mourning for all, beyond those within, will be comforted. Mourning is a part of the process of the work and working of all-inclusive love within the whole of life; mourning communities are open, receptive, softened – receptive to being comforted by communities who are embracing their instrumentality, who are instruments of all-inclusive love, instruments of the compassion of equality.

Blessed are the meek communities, for they shall inherit the earth. It is the way of working of humankind to come together in community in order to build structures and ways of structuring by and through which we feed, clothe, shelter, develop, educate, worship, govern, study, etc. Blessed are the meek communities, communities that take up their work from *Thy will*, not my will... intentional communities that embrace the aim of bringing the world of our making into congruence with the world of intent... communities meek... seeing that anything of value they bring into being comes from the life, love and wisdom of the Source. They are not the source, but instruments, intended instruments. The seeing of the way, the intended way, is available through meekness; meekness begins the process and enables the ongoingness of the process of participating with *the Father's eternalizing life commandment.* Meekness enters through seeing earth was created for life to have a place to enter into the working of the universe… seeing man was created for earth; earth was not created for man.

Blessed are the meek communities, for they shall inherit the living earth… they shall inherit the work, the roles and ongoing responsibility for joining with the Father in eternalizing life on this earth – now, at this time, the time of potential, the time of intent and intended ways, the time of the way of intent.

This seems a good place for pause and reflection. As we reflect on what has been written here, we see that the first beatitudes – the first four – are about preparing a community prepared for the work… a preparing which is ongoing, never ending… each beatitude being a process, an intended ongoing community process – the inner work essential for the process of each of the beatitudes that follow.

The second four are the processes of community entering into the world, community entering into our work, taking up our roles, in the world. And finally, the ninth, awakens us to the truth of what it means to follow *the truth of the way of life.* A deepening of truth that invites us to continue the process… to deepen our seeing, understanding and living as community poor in spirit, meek, merciful, peacemaking, virtuous, etc., community reciprocally nourishing within the whole of life. We can image an ongoing unfolding, an ever-deepening, ever-spiraling seeing, understanding, working… the way of becoming fully, truly and wholly human… as intended.

The Parable of the Prodigal Son (Lk15:1-32)…

In this parable, the younger son *squandered his inheritance on a life of dissipation…* a life of spreading, of dispersing, of squandering life. We each have access to gifts of the Source – the gift of life from the Life, the gift of the all-inclusive love Christ brought into life on this earth, and the gift of wisdom of the Spirit, the wisdom of intent and intended ways of life; intent being the essence virtue, the potential, the essence pattern imbedded when life enters. Such essence patterns enfolded and intended to be unfolded are imbedded in each and all members of life, and in life's systems and processes when life enters. We can choose to dedicate our lives to congruence with this intent, the intent of the Source, congruence being a co-operating with, fully participating in the unfolding of that which is imbedded – the unfolding of the enfolded virtue, by and through co-operating with the intended way of working of life. This is truly our inheritance… that which we – humanity, the people of earth – have been given by the Father, by the Source. our inheritance including the work we are called to take up, and the roles through which we are called to carry out the work.

The prodigal son *squandered his inheritance on a life of dissipation.* Not seeing himself as a member of life's family, a member of the life of the whole, of the whole of life, the prodigal son views all that he was given as something not so much as gift, but as right; not as truly belonging to the Father and for him to unfold in keeping with the intended eternal upwardly unfolding of life, the whole of life. And so, he used what he was given for his own personal desires – scattering and dispersing – not realizing, not making real, the purpose for which he was given life – and not embracing the truth of the Source from which that life came. He dissipated the gifts he was given; his life was in dissipation… ruins, wasted.

And he was wasting life itself. Scattering… dissipating life itself. Life moves us towards wholeness and oneness; dissipation separates, isolates, divides us from life. We can see and understand the Father declaring, *This son of mine was dead and has come to life again; he was lost, and has been found.* Here being dead is not a physical condition (although he was likely approaching physical death at an increasing rate), but a condition of the being and will that was dead, dead to the intent of the Life, the intent of Life for life, for the way of the ongoingness of life on earth; dead to the intentional purpose of life… dead as a member of the whole of life on this earth… dead to the intended work before him. We are either dead or we come to the Life, to life from Life. There is no "fence to sit on"; we are either consciously and conscientiously participating with, seriously intent on living from the intent and in intended ways of life… or we are not. We are either lost or we are found. There is no middle ground.

A Further Reflection…

Consider the brother who remained at home. We can be living "close to the Father," dutifully doing what we are told, and still not understanding and embracing our work and roles in fulfilling *the Father's command – eternal life, on earth as in heaven* (Jn12:50; Mt6:10) – not living from the all-inclusive love and not starting our thinking from the wisdom of the Spirit, the essence of that wisdom being required for intentionally working. All must consciously choose, choose to join with the Father in the work on this earth – the work of eternalizing life on this earth… always remembering, *if love – all-inclusive love – is not present in our process, love will not be present in the outcomes.*

158

When we listen to the *parable of the prodigal son* (Lk15:1-32) from the perspective of *the Father's command – eternal life on this earth* (Jn12:50; Mt6:10) – the whole of the story comes alive; the truth within the story is revealed. Our seeing develops as we listen as well from the perspective of work – intentional work and working – and from the perspective of community – it takes community to carry out intentional work.

The father's farm is the farm of life – the farm on which the unfolding of life is intended to become eternal. The farm takes community to operate... each having purpose, work and role in the ongoingness of the whole of life, the life of the whole. Consider the behavior of the prodigal son. He did not see this. He was looking from the perspective of existence as he asked for his inheritance – his part of earth's life resources – and squandered what he was given... dispersed and did not use them for the ongoingness of life. He separated himself from the garden; did not see himself as having an essential part in the ongoingness of life.

When he returned, the father was thrilled. The son had been dead... dead to life, and causing death to life. Now he was returning to his work, to take up his work and fill his role in the intended. Cause for celebration. He would no longer be dissipating life, no longer living a life of dissipation; and he would be with the father in the work of *the Father's command, eternalizing* life (Jn12:50).

The son who had been on the farm all along, although he was doing all that was asked of him, following the commands of his father, did not understand either. In some ways he might be called the "good" son... working on being good, being seen as good. Yet he still was more interested

159

in inheritance from an existence perspective than he was from the mind of essence, the mind of intent and intended ways. He was attached to punishment, not to forgiveness. He had not squandered life, but he had yet to, with all his heart, all his mind, all his spirit and all his soul, answered "Yes" to the work of the Father, answered "Yes" to intended ways of life, to the eternalizing life work.

Neither grasped the truth of the situation. It takes community to see and take up the work we inherit... the responsibility for the ongoingness of life on this earth. The intent was and is that we live in community, community taking up the work of intent and intended ways of life... work intended since the beginning of life entering earth. Our inheritance is not that which is handed over to us in existence, but the inheritance of the responsibility for life, for the intended eternal ongoingness of life on this earth.

We, each and all, whether we are the prodigal son or the good son, are now being called to enter into community, called to taking up intended work and role in the perpetuation of life on this earth. When we answer "Yes" to the work, this is a time for celebration of the Source... for we have been dead and have come to life; we were lost and have been found. Forgiveness is the beginning, not the end; forgiveness is the welcoming of us into the work... as we consciously and conscientiously choose to take up our work, our work in and with community, our particular work in the ongoing upward unfolding of life on this earth.

Blessed are the meek communities, for they shall inherit the earth (Mt5:5).

Blessed are the poor in spirit because of them is the kingdom of heaven (Mt5:3).

If I therefore, the master and teacher, have washed your feet, you ought to wash one another's feet. I have given you a model to follow, so that as I have done for you, you should also do. (Jn13:14-15).

The words of Christ, *Follow me* (Mt8:22), compel us to seeing Christ as process, as the intended way, leading to our reflecting on his words, his teachings, his life, death and resurrection, from a process perspective, the intended way of each and all of humanity for fulfilling our intentional purpose… Jesus providing the pattern of the process: *I have given you a model to follow, so that as I have done for you, you should also do.*

It seems we have a habit of reading much of what he said as speaking only of himself… or perhaps pertaining only to the disciples or those who have chosen the religious life. And yet, when we put on a new perspective, a life of the whole perspective, a process perspective from which we hear his words as leading and guiding the way of advancing our humanness, the way of becoming fully, truly and wholly human, as intended, we gain a fresh and true and life-giving insight to *following the way and the truth and the life* (Jn14:6). Leading to our seeing his words about himself from the perspective of their showing us the way for each of us taking up our work and role on this earth… words intended to come from our hearts and minds… words expressing the process, the way of intent, the way of our being and becoming intentional people.

All of which brings to mind, particular words of Christ: *Father, I glorified you on earth by accomplishing the work that you gave me to do* (Jn17:4).

When Jesus had risen, early on the first day of the week, he appeared first to Mary Magdalene... She went and told his companions who were mourning and weeping. When they heard that he was alive and had been seen by her, they did not believe.

After this he appeared in another form to two of them walking along on their way to the country. They returned and told the others; but they did not believe them either.

But later, as the eleven were at table, he appeared to them and rebuked them for their unbelief and hardness of heart because they had not believed those who saw him after he had been raised. He said to them, Go into the whole world and proclaim the gospel to every creature (Mark 16:9-15).

To whom did Jesus first appear? To the women... the women who had faith in Jesus, in Jesus' teaching, faith in *I am the way and the truth and the life* (Jn14:6); who believed in following the way, the process of Christ, the process leading to wholeness, the wholeness of family, community, people of earth, wholeness they were seeking. Women, who sat at his feet, trusted his words, and who could see the working of his process, see the coming together of people – people of all walks of life – see the transformation of healing, not only physically but in spirit. These women believed; and they saw the risen Christ.

He was seen by Mary Magdalene... and by two walking along their way in the country... two not named by Mark, Mark who carefully named Mary Magdalene – these two also women? The eleven – all of the living disciples – did not believe the women; did not believe that they had seen, what they had seen, what they had heard. Yet these two *were gathered in his name* (Mt18:20) were *gathered in the name of the way and the truth and the life*, gathered in the essence process of Jesus… a process with the presence of all-inclusive love. *If all-inclusive love is not present in the process; all-inclusive love is not present in the outcomes.*

Then Jesus rebuked the eleven; they still had not repented… had not changed mind and heart… and now the repentance, the change of mind and heart being called for, is the seeing and understanding of the whole of the truth of Christ and the opening of the heart to all-inclusive love.

And then he says, *Go into the whole world and proclaim the gospel to every creature.* Jesus did not say what he did not mean. How do we proclaim to very creature? How do we proclaim the gospel to every insect, bird, fish, animal? By living in harmony, congruence, co-operation with the original intent of the Source. Earth was created for life to have a place to enter into the working of the universe. This is the original intent and the ongoing intent of the Source… the intent of life on earth; and the intended ways of working of life itself. We proclaim the gospel to every creature by taking our part in fulfilling original intent… which includes proclaiming – through act – *the truth of the way of life…* act which proceeds out of taking up our (humanity's) intended purpose, work and role on this earth. Proclaiming the gospel only begins with teaching… from there requires intuiting… seeing the process and seeking wholeness within Christ, and obviously within life, as originally intended, since the beginning… seeing and seeking which opens us to the Spirit of Life, to the wisdom gifts of the Spirit.

Women blamed after the garden; women given the redeeming process after Christ – gift essential to everlasting life itself – women intended to lead the initiating process given us by Christ for the redeeming of humanity, redeeming possible after Christ completed the salvation work of then.

Women called to initiate with the mother's command –

Work for all my children, all children in the world.

Peace be with you (Jn20:21)... all-inclusive love be with you. If love is not present in the process, love will not be present in the outcome.

He breathed on them... Receive the holy Spirit (Jn20:22)... Spirit entering being essential to our seeing and under-standing the work of eternalizing life on this earth. We are unable, through the reasoning mind of existence, to "figure this out." Receiving the holy Spirit makes possible our speaking for earth by and through our work.

Whose sins you shall forgive are forgiven them (Jn20:23). Recall, Jesus asked, *Which is easier to say, take up your mat and walk, or your sins are forgiven?* (Mk2:9) Blind to our intended work and role in the eternal upwardly unfolding life on this earth, we are crippled, unable to walk the path of intent, unable to co-operate with intended ways of work-ing.

Whose sins you forgive are forgiven them... go into communi-ty – go into two or more gathered in the name of the all-inclusive love of Christ – and lead the creation of value adding processes... take an initiating role in the creation of value adding processes... creation of processes of value to the Source... processes that ongoingly add value to the intended eternal unfolding of life itself, on this earth, as the Father commands... processes fueled by all-inclusive love and initiated by virtue – intentional working, working in congruence with intent and intended ways of life.

Whose sins you shall retain are retained. In a world of our making void of Life, Love and Wisdom, we remain as the cripples on the mat... unable to walk, unable to take up our purpose, work and role.

My word shall not return to me void (Is55:10-11).

Take on an initiating role. Everything is in its place for this work.

Part 4

GOING FORWARD...
OR NOT

Our Story – Our Unfolding Story of Choice

I am in the Father and the Father is in me... I am in my Father and you are in me and I in you. Life is in me... I am the Life... and I am in you. Life is in you; you are in me (Jn14:6,11,20). Life is in all that we experience as living.

You must be born of water and the Spirit (Jn3:5).

Water is essential to the process of the Life entering earth... entering existence. This is the way of the process of the Life entering; creating that which, within existence, we call life, that which is living. *The Son of Man has nowhere to rest his head* (Mt8:20). Life entering earth is an intended ongoing process... each community of creatures of earth intended to take up our work and role in the eternal upwardly unfolding life. In the absence of such, life on this earth ends. Life must have receptive instruments to enter... instruments for fulfilling the intent of the Source and the intended way of working of life. All creatures on this earth are born of water. Water is the essential feature of earth that makes possible the ongoing entering of life into existence.

Spirit is essential to the fulfilling of the intended purpose, the intended work and role of humankind. *You must be born from above. The wind blows where it may, but you do not know from where it comes or where it is going. So it is with everyone who is born of the Spirit* (Jn3:8).

The honeybees, being members of life, are encoded to take up their work and role within the whole of life. In previous writings, we have visited the image of their working and particularly noted that if the honeybees were to stop pollinating, human life on this earth, all of life on this earth, would end in about four years. The work of humankind is also intended to reach beyond the ongoing sustaining of human life; humankind is intended to take a role in the eternalizing of life on this earth, in fulfilling *the Father's command of eternal life... on this earth as it is in heaven* (Jn12:49-50, Mt6:10). Unlike the honeybee and other creatures of life, we have choice.

And so, our story begins. We were created with choice; choice and decision being essential to the work before us. We, unlike the honeybees, have choice whether to co-operate with the entering of life into earth as intended, or to use that process for our own self, family, people. Giving humankind choice, the Source was painfully aware that we could choose our own powers of reason and reasoning over the wisdom of the Father, the Creator, the Source of all... and we could take a path of seeing self as source; turning away from wisdom, turning our backs on the Source, turning our backs on our "pollinating" role within the whole of life, even turning our backs on sustaining the hive of humanity.

And so we did; a choice and choosing we are continuing today. Only a short examination of conscience or moment of consciousness of the whole – the whole of humanity, the whole of life on earth of which humanity is a part – reveals this to ourselves about ourselves.

The Father provided us with commandments – rules of living together on this earth, so to speak – which, if we would even mechanically follow, would keep our communities together, would keep nations from destroying one another, until the coming of the hour of our choosing to return to the path of intent. Of course, this could not happen until at least one person on this earth – particularly a woman – would "return to the garden" – would embrace *one Source, all else instruments* and would give herself to the wisdom of the Source (versus the reasoning mind of man) to guide her thinking... one woman on this earth who would answer "Yes" to her intended work, without requiring a sign from God (as, for example, Zachariah did when the angel of God declared that his prayers were answered (Lk1:18))... one who turned her heart, her mind over to God... the first of humankind poor in spirit – who answered *Yes, do with me as you will* (Lk1:38)... a yes which held the most likely consequence of losing her life for the advancing of humankind. This is the baptism of water. *We must be born of water and the Spirit.* Being born of water calls for an entire, radical and permanent change of heart and mind... interestingly, not a change we make today and change back tomorrow... a change with no turning back; no looking back. Once Mary was pregnant, she was committed... a commitment with lifelong repercussions, consequences and responsibilities, including the possibility of giving up her life itself. *No greater love can man have for one another than to lay down one's life for one's friends* (Jn15:13). Do not forget that even if she got by without being stoned to death as was man's law at the time – the cultural law – she might not survive childbirth, the escape to Egypt, etc. She totally gave herself to the work God gave to her... without being told the future for herself; only the future, the purpose of her child. This was to be her work. *The wind blows where it wills, and you can hear the sound it makes, but you do not know from where it comes or where it is going.* Ours is not to know; ours is to have faith that if we answer "Yes" to our intended work and role, our intentional purpose, we will be given all that we need, everything will be in its place to take up our work, our calling.

This is metanoia; this life-changing decision of change, permanent change in mind and heart, which is to be made on pure faith, faith that if we choose this way, all that we need to fulfill our earthly obligations will be given to us, faith all we need to fulfill our "pollinating" work will be given us, is something called being born of water. Being born of water is a returning to the garden, embracing the living garden on this earth, and our intentional part in the whole of its working. At this time of potential, this time of now, being born of water is a community process (*two or more gathering in the name of Christ* (Mt18:20)), community answering "Yes" – yes to beginning all – beginning all thought, all thinking and therefore our direction and path – from wisdom, the wisdom of intent and intended ways of working of life; a yes given with faith, faith in intent; a yes embracing the truth:

> One Source, all else instruments, instruments choosing instrumentality within life (versus control over life)… we are intended instruments, intended for choosing instrumentality; intended members of life with work and roles in the intended eternal upwardly unfolding life.

Our work and role being particularly concerned with the upwardly unfolding part, for which we must fully participate in advancing humanness… advancing as humankind to a new world view… developing a new heart and mind which enables seeing and developing the intended human culture from the new world view, a culture within which we will become an intentional people of earth.

Having embraced this new living philosophy of potential, being baptized by water – *One Source; all else intended instruments; we humankind are intentional members of life with work and roles within life* – and having answered "Yes" to our instrumentality with all our heart, with all our mind, all our strength, all our soul, we are becoming a community prepared for assuming our work of sustaining human life, for sustaining the whole of life on earth. Always remembering that *God loves us* (Jn3:16) has a significant implication, that being, if love – all-inclusive love – is not present in our process, love will not be present in the outcomes… no matter how noble our efforts in the eyes of humankind. No matter the structures we have created on this earth; no matter the place in humankind's hierarchy we have taken or been given. All of which prepares us as a people prepared for the Spirit. This which we have just reflected upon is all essentially preparation work, the work of preparing ourselves for taking up the work of now. Preparation work being of the nature that when we look upon it, we say, "They are good people." We are *a people prepared for being born of Spirit* (Lk1:17).

As we reflect on the second birth, the being born of the Spirit, we see the raw truth of Jesus' words, *Why do you call me good? No one is good except one, God* (Mk10:18).

What we are calling good is like the honeybees working together for the sustaining of the life of the hive, producing and storing honey, building and cleaning the hive, reproducing, etc., all the while drinking sugar water; we are like bees failing to pollinate. And we know well, the end of that story.

Leading us to the work of developing an image of being born of the Spirit… work which may be helped by reflecting upon a prayer, a prayer familiar to many, one I have known since childhood…

> *Come holy Spirit,*
> *Fill the hearts of your faithful…*
> *Enkindle in us the fire of your love,*
> *And we shall be created…*
> *And you shall renew the face of the earth.*

… a prayer reminding us that we are to change, and through us the Spirit renews the earth. Our reflection is helped by returning to the dialogue between Jesus and Nicodemus... and recalling the words, *The wind blows where it may; we do not know from where it comes or where it is going. So too with the Spirit. We must be born of water and Spirit.* We have a word we use when the Spirit speaks to us; particularly when we hear the voice of wisdom and/or see intended ways of working of life, hearing and seeing of which we truly know we are not the source; that word being intuition... often referred to as women's intuition, not to be confused with the wisdom of experience which is the organizing into a whole that which we have experienced in and through life; although the intuition that comes through our experience develops the capacity for the process of intuition – the process of intuition being the process that opens our hearts and minds to the wisdom gifts of the Spirit. Referred to as women's intuition for it seems that experiencing intuition calls for dialogue, reflective and receptive dialogue on subjects of significance to life... the nature of process and processing most often found – when it is present in today's world – between and among women... a process held in diminishing value within our culture today; a process being diminished through technological inventions entering into our households and patterns of activity interrupting the dialogue and/or the potential for dialoguing (e.g., around the kitchen table, between mothers and daughters when preparing meals and doing household chores, among neighboring women processing the raising of the neighborhood children). Life itself is at risk should our society lose its last bit of capacity for reflective dialogue. For here is the truth... dialoguing – reflective dialoguing, intentional dialoguing – develops the essence mind of community, the mind receptive to the wisdom gifts of the Spirit: seeing what the reasoning mind of existence does not see; hearing what the reasoning mind of existence does not hear (Mt13:13-14). That which we are intended to hear, intended to see, is the intent of the Source and the intended ways of working of life – intent and intended ways, the seeing and hearing of which are gifts of the Spirit, gifts which enter the community mind of essence, the intuitive mind open and receptive to that which is available to all, made available by and through Jesus completing his work on this earth and sending the Spirit.

Pausing for a moment, we notice all of what is written here to be useful food for our reflective dialogue in our own community as we consider being born of water, that is turning hearts and minds – choicefully and permanently turning hearts to children and minds to virtue... at this time of now, the particular choice essential and called for being an advancing of the choice beyond the time of John the Baptist (Lk1:17), being that of turning our community hearts to pursuing that which works for all children in the world and turning our community minds to bringing into being a world of our making congruent with the world of intent – the world of Thy will being done on this earth at this time; both of which are essential to our moving towards wholeness, away from that which divides. This is the being born of water, community embracing life – the whole of life and life of the whole – and our role as community within life... this is community – like the honeybee hive – taking responsibility for the sustaining of the hive of humanity, a people prepared for ongoingly intentionally participating with the entering of the Spirit of truth... a people prepared for taking up our "pollinating work"... a people prepared for being born of the Spirit. Being born of the Spirit is not an event, but an intended ongoingly repeated process. Recall the honeybees. Their coming together in dance is not an event of the past, but an ongoing process of developing the mind now needed.

Being born of the Spirit: *hearing* the voice of intent; *seeing* intended ways of working of life; and *taking up our mat and walking* (Jn5:8). Through the wisdom gifts of the Spirit, the life of the Source and the love of Christ, we have all that we need to no longer be crippled/lame – self-serving and human centered. We can walk... walk the path of *Thy kingdom coming, Thy will being done on earth as in heaven*... the path of *sanctifying, hallowing, making whole the name of the Father*, the Source of all.

Recall Jesus chides Nicodemus, *You call yourself a teacher – you call yourself good – but you do not believe, you do not believe that the Spirit speaks to us, to the open and receptive; you have no faith. And if you do not believe it possible to hear the voice of the Spirit, then how will you ever (will you ever?) believe those who have heard, those who have seen?* (Jn3:10-12)

Let us return to the process of intuition by reflecting on processes during which mothers and daughters are developing the intuitive community mind of essence – the mind that sees process and is seeking wholeness – particularly one mother-daughter process, that being the time of working together in the kitchen. Capacity for intuition now needed is built through reflecting – in dialogue – on serious subjects... on life and the Source of life, on the word revealed and the works unfolding (the unfolding creation on earth). At this time of now, reflecting with the aim of seeing process – particularly seeing life as process and seeing Christ as process – and seeking wholeness – wholeness in seeing the essence pattern of Christ and wholeness in seeing the essence patterns embedded within life, wholeness in seeing intended eternal ongoingly unfolding life. Within our ways of today, we have the habit of neatly dividing, separating Christ and life from coming together in wholeness, as intended... since the beginning.

This building of the intuitive community mind of essence through ongoing reflective intentional dialoguing being essential to our openness to the Spirit of truth which enables our going out into the world, taking up our work and role in harmony and congruence with intended ways, with original intent. Without our "pollinating work," work possible through seeing intent and intended ways of life, we can sustain ourselves for a while – through extracting from and subduing life – but at this time of now, a time when earthly life itself is threatened by the world of our making, a time when children on earth are going hungry – physically, emotionally, spiritually – we may no longer turn our backs on the Source, the Life, no longer take ourselves as source; no longer depend on the reasoning mind of existence to solve the problems and issues we have created. Now is the time for being born of the Spirit: Taking up of the work, the seeing of which is given us by the Spirit (through the mind of essence and the intuition of wholeness), intentionally working in ways that are "pollinating," in ways that are reciprocally nourishing within the whole of life on this earth; reciprocally nourishing being essential NOW, in the here and unfolding now. Now is the time for our receptivity to intuition – the intuition of wholeness – the capacity we develop as we are preparing ourselves for becoming a people prepared for the Spirit entering, for being born of the Spirit.

All of which brings us to the words, *As the Father has sent me, so I send you. Receive the holy Spirit. Whose sins you shall forgive, they are forgiven them; and whose sins you retain are retained* (Jn20:21-23).

As the Father sent me; so I send you – two or more gathering in my name – into community to create processes of value… processes sourced in virtue – the intent of the Source and the ways of working of life intended by the Source – processes therefore capable of real value, value to the advancing of humanness, value to the intended eternalizing

179

of life on this earth... processes ultimately of value to the Source of all... processes which are the fulfilling of the ongoing manifesting on this earth of *the Father's command of eternal life on earth as in heaven. As the Father sent me, so I send you* into community, into becoming true community, community creating value adding processes... processes initiated by and through roles that embody all-inclusive love; the initiating process role of now being *intentional grandmothering.*

Whose sins you forgive are forgiven them; whose sins you retain are retained. The unforgivable sin being the sin against the holy Spirit (Mk3:28-29) – rejecting the wisdom of the Spirit or taking credit for the gifts of the Spirit and using them for self and human serving purposes (no love in the process). Forgiving sins being the process of community being born of water and Spirit – embracing, taking up and living by *the Father's command, eternal life on earth as in heaven,* being led by the wisdom of intent, the wisdom gift of the Spirit of truth, and fueled by all-inclusive love, the love of Christ, the love which manifests as compassion of equality.

Sins retained within humanity are within communities turning their backs on the Source, blaspheming, denying, closing out the Spirit and operating from me, mine and ours rather than with all-inclusive love in the process. Sinning retained in the one community is, of course, ultimately being retained within the whole of humanity... ultimately devastating all children of life... devastating all earthly life.

At this time of now, early words of the gospel come to mind... *Forgive us our debts; as we also forgive the debts of others.* As long as we feel others – persons, communities, ideological groups, nations, even life – owe us, are indebted to us, we are indebted to the Father, to the Source – to Life – the Source of life. As long as we are not forgiving of the debts of other communities, we are a community seeing ourself as superordinate to the other. There is only one hierarchy and that is the Source and there is all else, all else being equal in essence. As we forgive the debt of others, we move away from divisiveness towards seeing wholeness, wholeness of humanity, wholeness of life on earth; making possible our working for all children in the world, our working in congruence with intent and intended ways of working of life. An open forgiving community heart is the essential instrument for the entry of the all-inclusive love of Christ, for the compassion of equality to be manifested on this earth, the nature of love essential to our taking up our work, work of becoming reciprocally nourishing within the whole of life Hanging onto trespasses of others, debts of others, we hang onto a place of judging others; a place we were never given, a place we took at the time of original sin; a time when we turned our backs on original intent. Now, here and now, we are being given another way... a way that begins with the aim of rising above our stuckness in our goodness to embracing the yes of our instrumentality, to becoming communities gathering in his name, instruments of all-inclusive love, instruments of the compassion of equality, compassion which – with the wisdom of the Spirit – leads to open forgiving community hearts. For the quiet of wisdom of the Spirit shows us the intent of the Source – the virtue we are here to unfold – within the intended way of working of life – not our way, but the way intended by the Source since the beginning – a seeing that enables us to see real sin... sin against the Father's command; *eternal life... on earth as in heaven.*

As the Father has sent me, so I send you... Go into the world and proclaim the gospel to every creature (Mk16:15)... only possible with the ongoing wisdom gifts of the Spirit. True forgiveness – open forgiving community heart – makes possible the hearing of the voice and the seeing of intent... hearing and seeing which makes possible our living and working within and among life on earth… moving towards intent. Retained sins are those debts and trespasses communities cannot let go of; unable to let go, we are unable to see, to hear… we are crippled; unable to take up our work – original intent – the work of eternalizing life on this earth as in heaven.

Jesus is telling us we must become intentional people – people able to forgive. Retained sins are like a cancer within the whole of humanity, the whole of the life on this earth… retaining sins, we are spinning out from the intent of the Source; "drinking the sugar water" of being above others – while what is now needed is the compassion of equality; what is now needed is communities taking up our given work – the particular work of now on the path of eternalizing the intended upwardly unfolding life on this earth… with all our strength, with all our heart, with all our mind, with all spirit, with all our soul, living and working by the commandments Christ taught to be the essential three – *Love God; Love one another as I have loved you; Eternal life on earth as in heaven* (Mt22:37, Jn13:34, Jn12:49-50, Mt6:10).

We can hear Jesus speaking to us – rebuking and challenging: *Have faith the Spirit will speak to you… and to others as well. And always remember, work begins with washing the feet of each other, of all others; as I have done for you* (Jn13:14).

And so...

It is through seeing Christ as process that Christ enters into the world through us.

It is through seeing life as process that we enter into life.

It is when we are in process that we are manifesting the will of the Father.

It is the way of Christ to move towards wholeness, away from that which divides – the manifesting of all-inclusive love.

In moving towards wholeness we move towards truth; the ever deepening wholeness of truth... embracing truth versus reductionist arguing.

In moving towards wholeness we move into life, the Life, the whole of life.

To be of the Father, to be with Christ, is to be in process... in the process of the here and unfolding now... free of the structuring of the past, of the future... being present in and to the here and unfolding now.

To be of the Father, to be with Christ, is to be of and from the Spirit... living fully in a life of the Spirit.

Reflecting on the way of intentional grandmothering,

> We see process – life as process, Christ as process – at work...

> We see the realness, the potential for and in our living within this truth:

I am in the Father and the Father is in me.

I am in my Father and you are in me and I in you…

Life is in me…

I am the Life and I am in you.

Life is in you; you are in me (Jn14:6,11,20).

Life is in all that we experience as living …

And we see, through the active presence of intentional grandmothering, the forming of a culture, a culture that works for all children – all children in the living world.